IMPERATIVES AND THEIR LOGICS

IMPERATIVES AND THEIR LOGICS

Nicholas J. Moutafakis
The Cleveland State University

STERLING PUBLISHERS PVT LTD
NEW DELHI 110016   JULLUNDUR CITY

© 1975, *Nicholas J. Moutafakis,*

First Edition 1975

Printed in India

Published by S. K. Ghai Managing Director Sterling Publishers Pvt Ltd
Printed at Sterling Printers, L-11 Green Park Extn.,
New Delhi 110016

To my Father & Mother
DEMETRIOS
AND
SOPHIA MOUTAFAKIS

Introduction

A theme permeating contemporary philosophical thought is that of developing a logic of imperatives. From the late 1920's onwards the question of how to structure imperatives into an exact logic, and thus set forth a formal foundation for value theory, has engaged the efforts of linguistic analysts, both in Europe and in the United States. However, one characteristic of these attempts is the inability to find agreement upon even the elementary properties of imperatives. This difficulty seems to stem largely from the variety of interpretations imperatives are open to when viewed contextually. Furthermore, because of the close attention paid to the varieties of meanings imperatives have in context, a formidable problem is encountered by most in trying to handle imperatives within a two-valued propositional logic. In general, therefore, no successful logic of imperatives has yet to be devised.

The aim of this work is to explore these various attempts, and to determine the reason why they fail. Also, an attempt will be made to articulate a more acceptable logic of imperatives. For this purpose the book is presented in two parts.

The first part deals with the *prominent* attempt at articulating logics of imperatives, during the past half century. Within this part four chapters are set forth. Chapters I investigates the contributions of Ernst Mally and Karl Menger, who pioneer in the field of imperative logics. Their work is found to be lacking in so far as their conception of imperatives is not clear, so that their logics do not perform as intended. The second chapter deals more directly with the "proper" interpretation of imperatives, in so far as this was considered by positivists, who dismissed the cognitive meaning of imperatives *qua* imperatives. In contrast to the thorough reduction of imperatives to indicatives, a third chapter is presented. Here is discussed the opposition to the positivists handling of imperatives as indicatives. This comes to involve a deeper contextual analysis of how imperatives function in language. Finally, the major commentators of more recent times are taken up in the fourth chapter, where it is noted that a greater emphasis is placed on the power of logical techniques to capture the logic of imperatives.

All these attempts proceed mainly on the assumption that a sufficiently penetrating intensional analysis of imperatives will reveal the logical structure of imperatives in ordinary discourse. However, it turns out that these thinkers pay so close attention to the intension of imperatives that they cannot reach even the semblance of a logic to cover the many different aspects imperatives are found to have. There results, therefore, a general failure to arrive at a working logic of imperatives.

So as to circumvent some of the difficulties resulting from the intensional analysis of imperatives, the second part of this study is devoted to the articulation of a logic of imperatives through an extensional and pragmatic analysis of imperatives. This approach to the problem has not been carefully considerd by commentators. Moreover, what results is somewhat clearer conception of the relations which imperatives involve, and therefore a logic of imperatives arises which appears simpler and more acceptable than other such logics.

Accordingly, the second part involves chapters five and six. The fith explores the extension of imperatival discourse. Here an attempt is made to set down the ostensibly determinable extensional and pragmatic relations which imperatival discourse is found to have. The purpose of this investigation is twofold. First, it is geared towards the determination of the most prominent features of imperatives and responses to imperatives, so that some basic groundwork can be arrived at which can be publicly confirmed. Secondly, by bringing out the said relations one can easily handle imperatives and responses to imperatives sententially, something which proved terribly difficult for the intensionalists.

The sixth chapter builds from the epistemological foundation prepared in the previous chapter. It first sketches a formal language L, and then sets down some simple definitions and theorems pertaining to imperatives, as conceived from an extensional and pragmatic viewpoint. subsequently, a logic of imperatival events is presented, which is an extension of the logic of imperatives.

A concluding section of this chapter argues that the articulated logic is simpler and much more powerful than the logics presented by other. Here it is noted that in none of their attempts is there even an indication of the formal relations brought out in the proposed logic. Also it is seen that the problem of what to do with the emotive element of imperatives, which proved quite formidable to the intensionalists, never arises in the suggested logic of imperatives. Thus also the issue of the nature of imperative inference is no longer problematic, in that such inference is essentially an indicative inference.

The importance of formulating an acceptable logic of imperatives cannot be overstated. For as a basis for a theory of value, a logic of imperatives provides a means of rationally determining how value judgments, when taken as imperatives, relate to each other. Here one has a new field of investigation to explore, which involves not only Ethics, but also the Philosophy of Science, the Philosophy of History, and the Philosophy of Law.

However, the scope of this study is *only* the examination of the literature on the logic of imperatives, and the presentation of a logic of imperatives which is somewhat more useful than other such logics. Our own suggested logic is, nonetheless, tentative. It is meant only as an experimental investigation into the formal relations which xii

imperatives exhibit, when viewed from an extensional and pragmatic position.

I would like to express my appreciation to Richard M. Martin, who over the years has provided me with wise counsel as to the preparation of this manuscript. Special thanks are also due to Leslie Armour and Frederick Holck, who assisted me in the technical handling of the manuscript. Finally, I am deeply grateful to Miss Christina Tartal for her part in typing the final copy.

CONTENTS

PART II

SOME STEPS FORWARD

PART I

"HISTORICAL BACKGROUND"

1

The Early Attempts at Developing A Logic of Imperatives

Ernst Mally is first in presenting a fully articulated logic of imperatives. In this he seeks to illustrate an analogy between logical reasoning and willing, i.e. moral deliberation. However, his work in this connection, *Grundgesetze des Sollens*, has been largely neglected by commentators. Even Karl Menger, who claims to have considered Mally's contribution closely, disregards the basis upon which Mally develops his logic, and concentrates only upon the "logical futility" of the latter's main thesis that an imperative p is formally equivalent to the proposition that what p demands ought to be.[1]

Thus a study of contemporary attempts at developing a logic of imperatives properly begins with Mally's pioneering work. Moreover, Mally's position should be looked at from the point of view of its philosophical foundation, as well as from the view of the logic he seeks to articulate. It is part of the purpose of this chapter, therefore, to concentrate on both these aspects of Mally's contributions. Here it will become apparent that the major difficulty with his presentation lies not only in the formal proof he presents, but also in his adaptation of aspects of Franz Brentano's phenomenology, and refinements of it by Alexis Meinong.

Only when Mally's philosophical motives have been investigated, does Menger's objection become more understandable. Also, Menger's attempt to improve upon Mally's logic deserves consideration here as well, since his short proof of Mally's conclusion surpasses in clarity the overly complex proof given by Mally himself. Thus as a sequel, an exposition of Menger's contributions will be given. Of special interest is the extent to which Menger succeeds in presenting a more acceptable logic of imperatives than Mally. For Menger's attempt to include commands and wishes in a "logic of the doubtful" is fraught with ambiguities, among which is that it involves an ambiguous sense of "command."

Common to both Mally's and Menger's attempt is the idea that imperatives are *directly* translatable into some formal language. Thus the problem concerning the meaningfulness of imperative sentences, which shall prove an obstruction for the positivists, is not seen by either Mally or Menger. Both simply allow that imperatives deal with states of affairs, which form the basis for attributing truth-values to imperatives. Thus also, what these thinkers have to say is free from discussions dealing with the noncognitive status of imperatives, which again characterize the positivist viewpoint. In general, therefore, the "emotive" nature of imperatives is not seen by Mally or Menger as an impediment in inferring imperatives *qua* imperatives within some logic.

Section 1. **Ernst Mally's Logic of Imperatives** (der Logic des Willens)

Mally seeks to prove in *Grundgesetze des Sollens* that a proposition meaning that p is commanded is logically equivalent to the proposition that p ought to be true : '!p'. Moreover, the conclusion 'p≡!p' represents the vindication of the view that imperatives exhibit relations analogous to those of formal logic.[2] It follows, therefore, that an understanding of Mally's proof would be incomplete if the foundations for this analogy were not considered. Thus Menger's criticism of this conclusion, to the effect that the conclusion itself renders the symbol '!' superfluous, must put aside until the "philosophical justification" of Mally's thought is brought forth.

The examination of the latter involves considering the extent of Mally's indebtedness to Brentano. Evidence of Mally's reliance on the latter occurs variously throughout former's work. For he takes Brentano as a starting point insofar as Mally employs the idea of an analogy between ethics and logic, which is realizable only by inner reflection. Thus a few expository remarks are appropriate concerning Brentano's views on this analogy.

Frenz Brentano states in the *The Origin of the Knowledge of Right and Wrong* that logical laws are "naturally valid rules of judging," in that one is obliged to conform to them if he seeks certainty in his judgments. Furthermore, the "natural superiority" which one attaches to thought processes which conform to such laws, as opposed to those which do not, is also to be found in ethics, where one experiences a "natural preference" towards action which is directed towards the fulfilment of a definite desired end.[3]

While it is not purposeful to deliberate upon the plausibility of Brentano's subjectivism in ethics, it is pertinent to explore his conception of the will, as well as his analogy between logical reasoning and willing in a moral context.

The analogy indicated by Brentano is to be understood with respect to his classification of the faculties of mind. Basing the latter on various relations holding between a subject and an object, Brentano states that the relation of a subject having an idea is the simplest possible relation. This psychic phenomenon embraces all states dealing with love and hate, and the intermediates between these : willing, sorrow, hope, desire, etc.[4]

The ultimate justification he gives for the above classification is found in "inner experience." Brentano also bases his unification of the Ego, that is, the unification of the first two types of relation with the third, upon the insight revealed by inner perception. Such insight leads one to understand that holding an object to be true or false, as the result of making a judgment, is in essence, doing something *akin* to accepting or rejecting an object as being pleasant or unpleasant. For Brentano, the understanding which results from inner perception is the result of an exacting reflection, and not the result of introspection, which fails to distinguish between, for example, the mental act of imagining a colour and the mental act of actually seeing a colour. The fact of inner perception is the means whereby one sees the analogy between rational (or logical) judgment and desiring or willing some definite end.[5]

In another passage of this work, Brentano states more clearly the relation between an object and one's disposition towards it. He says that the subject matter of the moral and the immoral is the will. In most cases, what one wills is some definite means to an end. However, one wills the end also, and to a higher degree than the means. For it is the end alone which leads to other ends. Furthermore, man acts to achieve an end because he is motivated by a single end, which he esteems above all others. This highest end, (however it is conceived), insures the *rationality* of an individual's actions, since his behaviour is thoroughly characterized by the striving towards the achievement of this end.[6] The "natural preference," which Brentano takes as operating in moral conduct, arises because of the very *consistency of action*, which is necessitated by an esteemed end.

Of what importance to Mally is Brentano's analogy between the study of the will and logic? The answer to this question involves considering the extent of Mally's adaptation of Brentano's thought.

In the exegesis of the will Mally points out that to say that 'A must be' means nothing more than 'A is willed above all other things.' The relation between A being willed and A having to exist is to be understood in a dispositional sense, in that, when one is disposed towards willing something above all other things, one is disposed towards that thing as something which ought to be. In this connection, Mally refers to Brentano, indicating that he was the one who introduced and developed the idea of necessary being (*Seinsollen*) as predicated upon that which is willed.[7] In short, Mally says that the will arising from an end which is desired disposes one towards that end as that which ought to be. Hence for Mally, as well as for Brentano, the will arising from some end which is wanted manifests the necessity of the existence of that end.

Mally's indebtedness to Brentano is stated elsewhere in the above work. In his discussion of the relation between will and value, Mally says that whatever a person wills must be of some determinable value to him. And insofar as that which is willed must necessarily be, objective (*tatsachlich*) value is determinable with respect to the nature of what is willed. In this connection he refers to Brentano as the one who introduced the idea that there is an essential preference for the willing of some ethical good, since such willing is an action towards an esteemed end.[8] The "preference" here, following Brentano, is for action uniquely determined by the rationale of procuring the desired end.

Similarly, when considering what is a "proper" will, Mally also refers to Brentano. In clarifying the notion of "willing" he states that he is in agreement with Brentano that the highest (most proper) value is a "justified preference" (*berechtigtes Vorzichen*), rather than the commonly thought of strong demanding action (*starken Begehringsakt*).[9]

From the above it becomes evident that Mally's conception of the will follows that of Brentano's. Yet can it be said that Brentano's examination of the will by "inner experience" is sufficient to allow for Mally's presentation of a two-valued logic of imperative sentences? Though like Brentano, it is Mally's general objective to interrelate ethics and logic, one must first look at the way Mally conceives of imperatives, as objects of a formal language, before reaching a conclusion about how Mally adopts Brentano's analogy. For once the status of imperatives as objects of a calculus is clarified, then the nature of inference in Mally's logic can be judged in its proximity to formal logical inference.

Mally states in his introduction that he considers imperatives as "states of affairs" (*Sachverhalt*), in the sense in which Meinong speaks of "objects" (*Objekte*) in the latter's *Uber Annahmen*.[10] It is thus appropriate that consideration be given to Meinong on the above, after which Brentano's analogy, as employed by Mally, will be considered again.

In the work cited, Meinong looks at objects in two different ways. First there is the meaning of "object" as something which is judged to be the case. Here, "object" is a mental reflection directed towards some subject, whether real or imagined. Meinong often uses the work "*Gegenstand*" to refer to this kind of object. The peculiarity of this sense of "object" is that it does not involve an actually existing entity. For here Meinong includes both true and false judgments, assumptions, etc. Thus, such objects are phenomenological entities in a wide sense, and are more properly termed "objectives" rather than objects of immediate perception.[11] By way of illustration, the statement 'the sky is blue' contains the definite and distinct *circumstance* : "the-being-blue-of-the-sky." The latter (the objective) taken as an object (*Gegenstand*) is distinct from the perceived properties of the sky.

The second meaning Meinong attaches to the word '*Objekt*' is that of things being presented by ideas (*Vorstellungen*). In this sense, an "object" is not said "to be the case" in the sense that judgments or assumptions are said to reflect a "state of affairs" or circumstance. As J.N. Findlay remarks, Meinong considers this second sense of "object" as the *objectum* of that which the mind reflects upon as having a particular circumstance. Hence the *objectum* of the objective "the-being-blue-of-the-sky" is that *about* which something is thought, namely the sky.[12] Thus the sky is an object in the sense of that which is perceivable; while "the-being-blue-of-the-sky" is an object in the sense of *Gegenstand* : where one judges or assumes "that" such and such is the case.

Though Mally states that he is employing the word

Objekt in the same sense in which Meinong employs
it, it would be wrong to conclude that Mally refers to the
second sense of *Objekt* (that is object as *Vorstellungen*) when
speaking of imperatives as objects in a formal language.
At first sight it might seem simple to come to this conclusion, since Mally refers to Meinong's use of the word
Objekt, and the latter is used by Meinong almost exclusive-
ly for denoting the *objectum*. However, the following from
Mally's introduction suffices to show that it is the former
sense of '*Objekt*' to which he refers:

> ...wir urteilen dass etwas ist oder nicht ist, dass etwas
> so ist oder nicht ist, oder etwas, was im wesenlichen
> auf einer diesen Hauptformen gebracht werden kann.
> Sosein oder Nichtsosein, von irgend etwas, kurtz
> gesaght : ein *Sachverhalt*.[1] (my italics) Sachverhalt
> sind es aber auch, auf die das Wollen sich richtet: wir
> wollen, das etwas sei, nicht sei, so sei, oder nicht so
> sei. So kann es weningstens ausdrucken, wenn man
> hier wie beim Urteil von fieneren Unterschieden der
> Sachverhaltsform absiebt, die unsere Untersuchung
> ohne Berlang sind.[13]

In the above passage, Mally clarifies what he means by
"*Sachverhalt*" with a footnote to the effect that he intends
it to have the same meaning as Meinong's *Objekt*. However, that the second sense of this term is not meant, is
made clear by the fact that Mally, in the above passage,
compares the *state of affairs* (*Sachverhalt*) posited by judgments about things which may or may not exist, with *states
of affairs* posited by a willing or moral deliberation. Thus
the "imperatival" state of affairs should properly be termed
an objective (judgment) in Meinong's sense, rather than an
objectum. Mally's use of Meinong's notion of "objective"
enables him to consider statements dealing with imperatives
as statements having truth-value. This in turn makes it
easier to articulate imperatives in a two-valued propositional calculus. For imperative as "states of affairs" (*Sachverhalt*) are truth-functional to the extent that what is required
by an imperative is or is not satisfied: Thus Mally has

enriched Brentano's sense of will, which in the latter's case
is an "intuited" notion, so as to illustrate the logical nature
of imperatives.

Hence it can be seen that the analogy, which is hinted at
by Brentano, is brought out more vividly by Mally. For,
by considering imperatives as objectives in the same sense
as logical objectives, Mally attempts to prove the rational
nature of imperatives. In an exemplary passage he says :

> ...Auch das Wollen ist ein bestimmtes Stellungsnehmen
> zu Genestanden und es ist klar, das es auch hier
> Wesengesetze der Richtigkeit gibt : Gesetze richtigen.
> Wollens, die ihren Grundes Wesen als dieser bestim-
> mten Art des Verhaltnis zu Geneastanden haben. Und
> es ist klar, dass dieser Wesengesetze richtigen Wollen
> objectiv und rational sind im *demselben Sinne* (my
> italics) und aus *demselben Grund* (my italics) wie die
> logischen, und dass sie von allen empirischen, nur
> naherungsweise geltenden Gesetzmasigneiten willen-
> pyschologischer Art scharf zu unterschieden sind...[14]

In the above passage it is seen that Mally compares the
nature (*Wesengesetze*) of willing with that of formal inference, and observes that both are alike in the same sense
(*im demselben Sinne*) and for the same reason (*aus demselben Grund*). Thus at an early period Mally has begun to
think of imperatives and willing in general as a kind of
judgment that has a formal character akin to that of logical judgments. Without the earlier adaptation of Meinong's
sense of "Objekt" as "objective," however, the above
passage would be unclear. In short it is only because
Mally has elected to view imperatives as objectives, which
can be rendered true or false, that allows for the support of
the analogy between willing and logical reasoning.

Thus, Mally defends the above analogy not only on the
basis of Brentano's notion of "inner experience," which
accounts for the necessary existence (*Seinsollen*) of whatever
is commanded, but also on Meinong's notion of "objectives," which allows for attributing truth-values to

commands, and thus enables one to prove the analogy. Mally's conclusion : 'p≡!p', therefore, has a deeper significance than is ordinarily recognized. For once Mally's "philosophical justification" is explored, then the proof of his conclusion actually constitutes a proof of the analogy between the will and logic, as first mentioned by Brentano.

It is the proof of this conclusion within two-valued logic to which attention is now given; subsequent to which a criticism of Mally's entire thesis will be presented. Menger's short proof illustrates how Mally's conclusion can be arrived at without the complexity Mally's proof itself involves. On account of this convenience, Menger's proof will be employed to illustrate how Mally's conclusion is provable within a two-valued propositional logic, augmented by '!'.

Mally's conclusion 'p≡!p' states that where 'p' is a proposition meaning that something is commanded, then p is logically equivalent to the expression '!p', which says that what p commands ought to be.[15]

Interpreted in Menger's symbolism, Mally's primitives and postulates read as follows : '!p' stands for the proposition 'p ought to be true,' 'p' stands for 'non-p', 'p & q' stands for 'p and q is true,' 'p→q' stands for 'that p implies q is true', and abbreviating '(p & q)' and '(p→q) & (q→p)' by 'p→q', Mally's five postulates are expressed as :

(I) $[(p \rightarrow !q) \& (q \rightarrow r)] \rightarrow (p \rightarrow r)$

(I) reads : 'The conjunction of the implication that proposition p implies that the proposition q ought to be true and the implication that proposition q implies the proposition r implies the implication that proposition p implies that proposition r ought to be true.'

(II) $[p \rightarrow (!q \& !r)][\rightarrow]p \rightarrow !(q \& r)]$

(II) reads : 'The implication that the proposition p implies the conjunction of proposition p, which ought to be true, and proposition r, which ought to be true, implies the implication that proposition p implies the conjunction of proposition p and proposition r, which conjunction ought to be true.'

(III) $(p \rightarrow !q) \equiv !(p \rightarrow q)$

(III) reads : 'The implication that proposition p implies that the proposition q ought to be true is equivalent to the implication that proposition p implies proposition q, and which implication ought to be true.'

(IV) !u, which means, 'there is a proposition u for which !u is true.'

(V) '(!v)', which means, 'there is a proposition v for which the negation of !v holds.'

With the above Menger proceeds to give a proof of Mally's conclusion. Menger's proof itself, however, is stated in a laconic manner. Thus the proof given below fills out some of the steps Menger's proof assumes.

1. $!q \rightarrow !q$ ((Theorem of the propositional logic))

2. $!q \rightarrow ((!q') \rightarrow !q)$ ((Theorem of the propositional logic))

3. $p \rightarrow (q \rightarrow p)$ ((Theorem of the propositional logic))

4. $(p \ \& \ !q) \rightarrow \{(!q \rightarrow !q) \ \& \ ((!q') \rightarrow !q) \ \& \ (q \rightarrow p)]$ ((1,2 and 3))

5. $(p \ \& \ !q) \rightarrow !p$ ((Postulate I, step : 4.))

6. $(q \rightarrow !p) \equiv (q \rightarrow p)$ and $!(p' \rightarrow q') \equiv (p' \rightarrow !q'')$
             ((Postulate III, 5))

7. $(q \rightarrow p) \equiv (p' \rightarrow q')$ ((Theorem of the propositional logic))

8. $(q \rightarrow !p) \equiv (p' \rightarrow !q')$ ((steps : 6 and 7, and the Rule of Deduction))

9. $!p \rightarrow ((q \rightarrow !p) \ \& \ (q' \rightarrow !p))$ ((Theorem of propositional logic))

10. $(!p \rightarrow ((q \rightarrow !p) \ \& \ (q' \rightarrow !p))) \rightarrow (!p \rightarrow ((p' \rightarrow !q') \ \& \ (p' \rightarrow !q)))$
             ((steps : 8 and 9))

11. $p' \rightarrow (!q \ \& \ !q')$ ((step 10, implication))

12. $p' \rightarrow !(q \ \& \ q')$ ((step 11 and Postulate II))

13. $(p' \rightarrow !(q \ \& \ q')) \rightarrow [(p \rightarrow !(q \ \& \ q')) \ \& \ (!(q \& q') \rightarrow r]$
                                     ((step 12., implication))

14. $p' \rightarrow !r$ ((step 13, and Postulate III))

15. $(p' \rightarrow !r) \equiv (p' \rightarrow (p \ v \ !r))$ ((step 14, (equivalence))

16. $(p' \rightarrow (p \ v \ !r)) \equiv (p \rightarrow (p \ v \ !r))$ ((equivalence of $(p' \rightarrow (p \ v \ !r))$))

17. $p \rightarrow (p \ v \ !r)$ ((steps: 15 and 16, and Rule of Deduction))

18. $p \rightarrow !p$ ((step 17, and Postulate IV))

19. $!p \rightarrow p$ ((step: 18, and Postulate V)

20. $p \equiv !p$ ((steps 18 and 19 equivalence))

The conclusion $p \equiv !p$ represents for Mally the logical
nature of wishing or of commands. For this conclusion
says that there is a "logical equivalence" between 'p,' which
is a proposition stating that something is wanted or commanded by someone, and '!p,' which says that whatever is
the object of demand in p ought to be (*Seinsollen*). Thus
the entire expression $p \equiv !p$, plus the fact that it is provable
in a two-valued calculus, constitutes the vindication of
Brentano's thesis that there is a relation, analogous to a
relation of equivalence in formal logic, between the act of
willing (or commanding) and that which is willed (or commanded) ought to be.

Considered in the context of Mally's thought, the above
conclusion is a short means of expressing a view concerning the nature of the will. Thus in referring to Mally's
conclusion, one only partly understands it if he considers
just the formal proof of this conclusion, and not that which
the conclusion is intended to illustrate. For example, one
would fail to understand that in its full meaning this conclusion expresses a judgment in the sense that it expresses a
"state of affairs" (*Sachverhalt*), resulting from willing or
demanding something.

Has Mally succeeded in showing an analogy between
imperative reasoning and logical reasoning? His reliance
on Brentano is not sufficient to prove this. For it is
fundamental to Brentano's position that the "inner percep-

tion" which reveals the purported relation between logic and willing is solely subjectively evident. Here one would have to face the difficulties of subjective verification before accepting the above analogy.

Fundamentally Mally bases the analogy between willing and logical reasoning on the very proof he goes through to illustrate p≡!p. Thus the proof becomes an objectively determinable means of showing that logical reasoning and moral reasoning (willing) are analogous. The question now arises of whether or not Mally's proof serves the purpose he conceives for it.

In itself the proof in question only illustrates that the statement that p is equivalent to !p is deducible in a formal language. However, Mally does not construe his proof only as a means of proving a formal equivalence. Rather, he sees his proof as a "vindication" of the proposition that whatever is willed ought also to be (*Seinsollen*). In other words, the proof actually explains why when something is willed it ought to be as well. Though this may be Mally's interpretation of the formal proof he presents, it is hard to accept the view that a formal proof can really say anything more than that some statement is deducible in a calculus. To so interpret Mally's proof begs the question as to whether the steps of a sound proof can serve any other purpose than that of arriving at the conclusion of a chain of reasoning. Thus, at the very least, a problem exists as to how a formal proof can "vindicate" the observation by "inner experience" that whatever is willed ought to be as well. Mally, however, does not stop to consider the possibility of this issue.

More significantly, Mally's conclusion itself is beset with difficulties. For example, imperatives for Mally are seen as objectives in the sense explained. By this he believes himself able to attach truth-values to imperatives, since if the state of affairs alluded to by the imperative is the case then the imperative is to be taken as "true." However, he has not explained how the satisfying of an imperative makes an imperative true. The problem here is in attributing truth or falsehood to imperatives. Usually, a statement is said to be true or false because it is supported or not supported by facts. Yet, imperatives do not assert anything which can be substantiated by facts. Hence the question emerges as to how the values of truth or falsehood can be attributed to imperatives.

Mally's argument is that by satisfying or not satisfying an imperative one can regard that imperative as true or false. However, this argument is deceptive. For the satisfaction of an imperative in no way accounts for the objective truth of the imperative. Moreover, it makes no sense to speak of the objective truth of an imperative other than that the imperative was or was not given by some imperator. The determination of the authorship of an imperative is a different issue than that of whether or not the imperative has been satisfied. Yet even when the problem is the determination of the authorship of the imperative, it cannot still be said that an imperative is true or false because it has or has not been issued by the proper imperator. Rather, what the proper authorship of an imperative provides the truth for is the *sentence* that some imperative was or was not given by some imperator. Thus Mally has not shown how imperatives themselves can be handled in a two-valued logic.

In essence Mally has only shown that the statement 'p≡!p' is provable in a suitable two-valued propositional logic. However, he believes he has demonstrated that there is an analogy between the issuing of an imperative and logical reasoning. In this way also he thinks he has secured a logical foundation for imperatives. He would have succeeded in what he attempts if he could show that p,≡!p' *is* an imperative. For to secure the analogy Mally believes holds between imperative reasoning and logical reasoning one would have to treat the conclusion he draws as not predicating anything, but as in some way imperatizing that p is equivalent to !p. One sees, however, that once the imperative mood is considered in its full meaning, then there emerges the question of how a logic, intended so as to make possible the deduction of indicative statements, is able to prove anything about imperative sentences. At least there ought to be some intimation of a problem in translating imperatives into indicatives. On this point Mally assumes that there is no difficulty in going from indicative reasoning to imperative reasoning. It is because of this assumption, moreover, that Karl Menger seeks another approach to a logic of imperatives.[16]

Also, it can be shown that Mally does not distinguish between 'p' the command, '!p'='what p commands ought to be true,' and 'Op'='p ought to be.' In Mally's conclusion there is no way of distinguishing between these three different senses of 'p', since all three senses are taken as mutually dependent. Thus if 'p' is a command, then because p is a command it ought to be or Op, and *that* which is commanded ought to be or !p. Thus there is a confusion as to how Mally's conclusion can differentiate between these three distinct senses of 'p'.

Once Mally's conclusion is seen to be predicative and not assertive, then Menger's criticism of Mally appears more cogent. The superfluity of the symbol '!', to which Menger correctly draws attention, results from what Mally's conclusion predicates. For, according to his conclusion, 'p' alone means '!p'. Thus nothing new is added to 'p' with the introduction of '!' in front of 'p', and thus '!' can be introduced or cancelled anywhere within a formula of Mally's system. Menger, however, does not explain how the predicative function of Mally's conclusion, by not being an imperative, serves to undermine Mally's aim of showing the rational nature of imperatives. Menger only says that, since it renders '!' superfluous, Mally's conclusion is useless.

In summary, Mally's failure to present an adequate formalization of imperatives stems largely from preconceptions concerning their nature. His adherence to Brentano's analogy between the will and logic evidently precludes the issue that imperatives are logical in nature. It is thus not a question of the correctness of his logical proof that is at issue, but rather a question of whether Mally is correct in conceiving of imperatives as he does. As is indicated, the justification for considering imperatives in Brentano's manner lies in individual subjective experience. Thus there is always a methodological difficulty in showing how such experience is sufficient to demonstrate the purported analogy between the will and logic. For any statement Mally makes concerning the logical inference which imperatives are shown to involve is always suspect to the charge that he has not shown how imperatives have a rational nature. His proof that $p \equiv !p$ is no defence, since it turns out that '$p \equiv !p$' is not an imperative but an indicative statement. The logical nature of imperatives thus is not explicated by Mally.

Nevertheless it is important to point out that one should not abandon the attempt to formulate a logic of imperatives in a two-valued propositional calculus on account of Mally's failure. For it is possible to articulate a logic of imperatives within such a calculus, if imperatives are viewed differently. However, further discussion as to how this may be done will be deferred until later.

Menger attempts to improve upon Mally's thesis by presenting a logic of imperatives which avoids considering imperatives as either necessities or impossibilities. For Menger, commands and wishes are too complex to be contained and expressed within a two-valued propositional calculus.

Section 2. Menger's Many-valued Logic of Imperatives

Two aspects of Menger's work will be discussed. First attention will be given to how he conceives of imperatives, and whether this conception is acceptable. Secondly, the foundation of Menger's logic of the "doubtful" is to be examined. For not only are there serious difficulties in accepting this foundation, but there is also a question about the sense in which Menger's "logic" is an *alternative* to a two-valued propositional calculus.

A. *Menger's Notion of Commands*

In his article "A Logic of the Doubtful, On Optative and Imperative Logic," Menger states that the "objects" of commands and wishes are *"neither necessities nor impossibilities."* He stipulates that commands and wishes are to be dealt with as neither asserting nor denying anything, but should be considered as doubtful propositions.[17] This is as far as Menger goes in explaining what he means by commands and wishes.

However, what does it mean to say that an imperative is neither an assertion nor a denial? If Menger grants that the object of an imperative is what is demanded of the subject to whom the command is directed, then it must in some way be indicated that that which is commanded must or must not be the case. Yet if this is accepted, then commands cannot be taken as non-asserted or non-negated propositions. Thus there is a vagueness as to what Menger means by the "object" of a command. Furthermore, there is confusion in his saying that the object of a command must be a proposition. For according to him such a proposition is an uncertain (or doubtful) statement, since it is neither impossible nor necessary. Yet when one commands that such and such be done, one is explicitly stating that he wants such and such *to be* done. If this were not the case, and in fact the proposition stating what one wants is uncertain, then the command would be pointless, in that an agent could not act upon it. Also if commands are taken in Menger's non-asserted or non-negated sense, the imperative mood of imperatives cannot be accounted for. In short there would be no sense in which the immediate sense of urgency, which imperatives uniquely manifest, could be explained in Menger's terms.

Continuing, Menger proceeds to distinguish between the "formal properties" of commands and those of wishes. He states that according to the ordinary use of "command", a person may command p and he may command q, or both. To command both p and q may also mean that one commands p and q individually. On the other hand, according to the ordinary use of "wish," when a person wishes for p and q, or (p & q), it does not ordinarily follow that he wishes for p and q individually. He notes that the less discriminating nature of wishing is also illustrated by the fact that when two or more things are wished for they are always "complementary goods."[18]

The above distinction is brought out again by Menger, in terms of what he calls the "*implicational interpretation of attitudes*." He interprets the statement 'I command p,' or Cp, as "unless p, something unpleasant will happen (e.g. I shall get angry, or you will be punished)." Thus, using the symbol 'A' to range over all the unpleasant things that will happen, he writes 'Cp$\equiv$(p'$\rightarrow$A)', where 'p' 'means' —p', or 'not —p'. Employing the calculus of propositions, he arrives at '((p & q)'$\rightarrow$r)$\equiv$((p'$\rightarrow$r) & (q'$\rightarrow$r))', where 'r' is put in place of 'A'. This last formula is found to result in 'C (p & q)$\equiv$ (Cp & Cq)', which again shows that to command (p & q) implies the commanding of p and q individually.[19]

The implicational interpretation of wishes fares differently from that of commands. Symbolizing the statement "I wish 'p' as 'Dp' (where 'D' stands for 'desire'), Menger translates 'Dp' as 'If p, then I shall be glad!' Thus, denoting by 'B' the statement 'I shall be glad,' he writes 'Dp$\equiv$(p$\rightarrow$B)'. Employing the calculus of propositions, Menger arrives at '((p$\rightarrow$r) & (q$\rightarrow$r))$\rightarrow$((p & r)$\rightarrow$r)'. Thus applying the rule where 'B' is substituted for 'r', he comes out with "(Dp & Dq)$\rightarrow$D(p & q)'. Menger notes that because of the "common" use of the notion of 'wishing,' it cannot be proven from this last formula that to desire p and q jointly implies the desiring of p and q individually or 'D(p & q)$\rightarrow$ (Dp & Dq)'. However, in the case of commands it is seen that the common usage does allow the inferring of 'C(p & q)$\rightarrow$ (Cp & Cq)' from '(Cp & Cq)$\rightarrow$C(p & q)', as already indicated. In this respect, therefore, commands differ from wishes.[20]

In view of the above, it is constructive to consider what Menger has thus far contributed towards explaining his conception of commands. His view that according to the "ordinary use" of the word "command" two propositions may be commanded jointly or individually, leaves one to assume that he is paying attention to the function of ordinary language in his presentation of the nature of commands. Also, in his second illustration of the differences between commands and wishes, he considers commands as expressing or implying exhortations that if p is done or is not done, then the one uttering the command will get angry, or the one to whom the command is directed will be punished. The reader is again left to conclude that the exhortative meaning of commands is also the result of investigating the function of the word "command" in ordinary discourse.

However, it is not at all clear how Menger can claim that imperatives are basically doubtful propositions. For if he means that imperatives are doubtful because it cannot be known whether they are to be properly fulfilled, then the imperator's *intention* in giving imperatives becomes difficult to characterize. In the ordinary language context in which Menger speaks there is the tacit understanding that an imperator gives an imperative because he believes the agent addressed can bring about what is desired. If the imperator did not assume something about the agent's powers in carrying out the imperative, then the very purpose of issuing the imperative is lost. However, to assume that the agent is able to bring about what the imperator commands makes the imperative less doubtful than Menger is willing to grant. Moreover, within ordinary language use the observed assumption is not extravagant, and it illustrates the artificiality of Menger's conception of imperatives.

On the other hand, if Menger means that imperatives are doubtful because they neither assert nor deny anything, then the exhortative nature of commands becomes problematic. For it makes little sense for Menger to hold that imperatives do not assert, and yet maintain that the distinctive features of imperatives is that they involve some admonition towards the agent.

Menger next goes on to argue for the inadequacy of

propositional logic in handing commands and wishes. He says that the logic of propositions yields :

$$'((p' \to r) \& (p \to q)) \to (q' \to r)',$$

for any 'p', 'q', or 'r'. Applying this formula to 'r=A', he arrives at '(Cp & (p→q))→Cq', Menger indicates that an absurdity results if the propositional calculus is applied to this last result. First, if one commands a true proposition p, then he commands each true proposition q, since p→q, if both p and q are true. Also, if one commands a false proposition p, then he commands each proposition q, since p→q for any q if p is false. Here a paradox results, since, if it is assumed that each proposition is either true or false, any proposition which is commanded has to be either true or false. Thus a proposition which is commanded has to be either a false proposition (and thus any proposition), or a true proposition (and thus all true propositions).[21]

Menger considers this reason enough to commence upon a presentation of imperatives within a logic of the doubtful. The paradox, however, presupposes acceptance of his way of interpreting imperatives implicationally. The plausibility of this arugment is nonetheless open to question, since Menger does not consider the possibility of interpreting commands differently. For, in most cases, not every command implies another command. With respect to imperatives, implication is properly a secondary attribute. Certainly the disjunctive nature of imperatives, is so far as it becomes manifest in the simple satisfaction or non-satisfaction of what is commanded, is fundamentally of more concern than the implicational nature of commands. Implication is pertinent for study at a more advanced stage of dealing with imperatives, that is, at a stage where the structure of imperatives has been fully described, and *complex commands* are then considered. Thus, Menger's attack upon a two-valued logic of imperatives, because of its failure to explain imperatival implication, disregards the fact that his conception of commands is not at all clear, and it is therefore premature for him to venture into the implicational nature of imperatives without first clarifying how he conceives of commands.

B. *Mengers Logic of the Doubtful*

Menger's logic of imperatives is based upon his notion of "doubting." Indicating that imperatives are not adequately expressed in a two-valued logic, he seeks to deal with them in a broader calculus. The latter is provided by introducing the notion of "doubt" as a common dominator for reducing statements about commands and desires. Apart from the linguistic problem of reducing commands to probable (i.e. doubtful) statements, Menger's reliance on a logic of the doubtful, which is essentially a logic expressing wishes, is not advantageous.

Setting down the symbolism for three modal classes : assertion : 'M+', negation : 'M—', and the doubtful : 'Mo,' Menger gives three theorems from the following two assumptions : "(1) M+ is a deductive system in Tarski's sense, that is to say, a system containing each proposition that follows from any set of propositions of the system," and "(2) if p belongs to M+, then p' belongs to M—, and conversely."[22]

Since the foregoing assumptions are basic to Menger's "logic of the doubtful," an analysis of their plausibility is in order. It may be asked what Menger's intention is in saying that M+ is a deductive system in Tarski's sense. From what Menger has said thus far, M+ is the modal class of all asserted propositions, and, in view of his reference to Tarski, M+ is also a deductive system. Yet Tarski's position on deductive systems generally is that the two-valued system is really the only consistent system, and that the socalled alternative logics include aspects of a two-valued system, and are thus not really "alternatives" to a two-valued Logic at all.[23] Certainly, it cannot be said that the Menger can accept the position that a proposition with an imperative content follows from a set of propositions in the same manner as propositions are said to be deduced from other propositions in a deductive system featuring two truth-values. For M+ is primarily part of a non-two-valued logic, which Menger terms a "logic of the doubtful," and which includes, though as exclusive modal classes, M— and Mo. Also, Menger seeks to completely differentiate his logic from a two-valued propositional logic, or any other kind of logic which somehow includes a two-valued logic. Thus the reference to Tarski's sense of a deductive system, is obscured by Menger's refusal to include any aspect of a two-valued logic in "the logic of the doubtful." For these reasons there is a disturbing vagueness as to what Menger means where he says that M+ is a deductive system in Tarski's sense.

The obscure statement Menger attributes to Tarski, without referring it to any of Tarski's works, seems also erroneous. For a system which has each of its propositions follow from *any* set of proposition would be unworkable. In such a system one could presumedly have two contradictory propositions which follow from the *same* set of propositions of such a system. This much seems to be implied by Menger's first assumption that in a deductive system each proposition is derived from any set of propositions within this deductive system. Yet he seems to have overlooked the fact that in a *consistent* deductive system, one of two contradictory propositions must not be provable from any set of propositions of that system, though both contradictory propositions are *expressable* in this one consistent system.

Menger's second assumption is also difficult to accept, since it too assumes some aspects of a two-valued propositional logic, which he is trying to stay clear of. How else is one to interpret his assumption that..."If p belongs to M+, then p' (or —p) belongs to M—, and conversely ?" Here there seems to be the implicit assumption that modal class M+ and modal class M— are differentiated on the basis of the notions of true and false of the two-valued propositional logic. This is seen from the fact that he employs p and —p to illustrate how each of these classes relate to each other. Thus this distinction is made on the

basis of fundamental notions of two-valued logic. Hence
Menger is assuming this latter logic as basic to his logic of
the doubtful, though he outwardly opposes such an
assumption about his logic.

Furthermore, it now becomes difficult to see how Menger
can maintain that M+ and M— are mutually exclusive
modal classes, when he is seen to distinguish them on the
basis of the ordinary two-valued logic. For a serious
question arises as to how Menger's modal classes are to be
taken as "modal."

Menger's third theorem is perhaps of special interest,
since it illustrates the actual workings of the logic of the
doubtful, in contrast to a two-valued logic. The theorem
reads : "There are at most seven classes of pairsof doubtful
propositions. If $M(p)=M(q)=Mo$, then the modalities of
'p & q', 'p&q", 'p' & q', and 'p' & q", have one of the
following quadruple values :

p & q	p' & q'	p' & q	p & q'	and we say	and write
—	o	o	o	p and q are incompatible	piq
—	—	o	o	p and q are contradictory	poq
o	—	o	o	p and q are alternative	paq
o	o	—	o	p is weaker than q	pwq
o	o	—	—	p is stronger than q	psq
o	o	o	—	p is equivalent to q	peq
o	o	o	o	p is unrelated to q	puq."[24]

For example, the above table illustrates how the incom-
patibility of p and q arises from the negation of the
conjunction of p and q, the "doubtfulness" of the conjunction of the negations of p and of q, the "doubtfulness" of
the negation of p conjuncted with q, and the "doubtfulness"
of the conjunction of p with the negation of q. The other
values of the tables are to be read in a similar way.

However, it should be kept in mind that according to
Menger, (yet contrary to what is the real case), the symbol
'—' does not stand for "negation" in exactly the same sense
in which this notion is used in the two-valued propositional

logic. Rather, in the context of his thought, '—' is taken in some sense *as contrasted to* assertion : '+' and the doubtful : 'o'. Though Menger is not at all clear as to the exact meaning of his primitives, it appears that propositions (in Menger's sense) prefixed by '—' are to be regarded as non-assertable propositions, but which are also of a sufficiently ostensively determinable nature so as not to be doubtful, or 'o' propositions. Thus, in turn, a doubtful proposition is one which is neither an assertable or '+' proposition, nor a non-assertable or '—' proposition. Here, however, an added complication results by the fact that Menger often refers to his doubtful propositions as "possibly" asserted or "possibly" non-asserted. Thus one cannot treat Menger's doubtful propositions as completely separate from assertable propositions, whatever he means by "propositions." In this connection, one has to consider the even more problematic notion of a sentence (or proposition) which is neither asserted nor non-asserted.

Menger says that the above modalities reflect the "logic of everyday life," and that in this logic, unlike other logics, the class of the compound is not uniquely determined by the classes of the components. For the propositions : 'Tomorrow it will rain,' 'Tomorrow it will snow,' and 'Tomorrow it will not rain' are all doubtful propositions. Thus 'Tomorrow it will rain' is not necessarily the "contradictory" of 'Tomorrow it will not rain.'

Because of the "doubtfulness" of all propositions in Menger's logic, an uncertainty results in the way one is to understand the fundamentals of his logic. For if one goes along with Menger's view that the assertion of the proposition is not the contrary of the negation of that same proposition, then how is one to construe Menger's second assumption that "If 'p' belongs to M+, then 'p' or (non-p) belongs to M—, and conversely ?" This assumption clearly equates '+' and '—' with ordinary two-valued logic truth and falsehood respectively. Yet elsewhere Menger is shown to distinguish the assertive '+' modal class from the negative '—' modal class by means of the doubtful modal class. Also, it is seen by such examples as : 'Tomorrow it will rain,' and 'Tomorrow it will not rain,' that all propositions are doubtful in Menger's logic. However, if this is granted, then how can Menger include any proposition in either the assertive, non-assertive, or even doubtful modal class ?

Furthermore, what does it mean to say that the logic of the doubtful is the "logic of everyday life ?" What is the logic of everyday life ? If he refers to the ordinary use of language as the logic of everyday life, then he is seriously mistaken. Linguistic usage is based upon conventions, which reflect few formal relationships. Also, the very advantage of a logic is that it provides for treating propositions in a precise manner, which is lacking in ordinary language. Thus it is uncertain what Menger means by the "logic of everyday life." Here, as in the case of the former objections, obscurity in his laconic style makes it difficult to grasp Menger's meaning.

Finally, Menger says that his logic of the doubtful is different from the many-valued logics because of the indicated doubtfulness of all propositions expressable within his logic. Yet to what extent is Menger's system a "logic?" By saying that his system is in some way different from other logics, Menger is assuming that his system is a logic, though in an expanded sense of the term. This new meaning for the word, however, allows that a given formal system need not be reflective of precise reasoning. This follows from the simple fact that no proposition in Menger's logic is ever certain. On the other hand, complete rational certainty is ordinarily taken to be the goal of logical reasoning.

In view of this, why is a logic such as the one proposed by Menger an "alternative" to a two-valued propositional logic of imperatives ? Menger does not prove that his logic of the doubtful is totally different from other kinds of logic. The fact that he considers his system a logic, in which logic equivalence is defined as in ordinary two-valued logic, indicates that aspects of the latter logic are somehow included in his logic of the doubtful. Nor does Menger deny that the logic he presents contains a two-valued logic. However, if it is the case that two-valued logic does form a part of the logic of the doubtful, then Menger's logic is no alternative to a two-valued logic of imperatives, assuming that one can be successfully formulated. However, Menger is silent on the extent of influence that a two-valued logic has on his system.

Menger's attempt is thus seen to suffer from a vagueness as to what imperatives mean, as well as from a lack of precise definition of the essentials of his system. Thus there results a highly artificial presentation of imperatives, which makes Menger's system useless as an analytical tool. As in the case of Mally's use of the idea of the "obviousness of imperative rationality," so also with Menger's appeal to "everyday logic," there is assumed a certain self-evidence about the nature of imperatives. This assumed simplicity of the nature of imperatives is seriously challenged by subsequent analysis of prescriptive discourse.

What has resulted from this discussion is an understanding of the types of the problems one gets into in attempting to formalize imperative sentences. Certainly Mally's failure to successfully render imperatives within a two-valued logic reflects a deep difficulty in managing sentences of the imperative mood as indicatives. Similarly, Menger's inability at capturing the logic of imperatives by means of introducing new primitives in a logic of the so-called "doubtful," illustrates the illusive meaning of imperatives when viewed contextually. Furthermore, such problems form the source of difficulty for future attempts.

2

The Analyses of Imperatives

Discussions dealing with imperatives come to involve the "meaningful content" of imperatives, as positivism influences thinkers. It is part of the purpose of this chapter to bring out what the aims of the positivists were in treating imperatives as linguistic entities, which do not assert anything, and which only express feelings. In this connection the epistemological foundations of positivism will be considered as they appear in the pertinent works of Rudolf Carnap, Moritz Schlick, A.J. Ayer, and C.L. Stevenson. These men prepared the way for a trend appearing in the late thirties and early forties, which stated that a logic of imperatives apart from the logic of indicatives was impossible because of the noncognitive nature of imperatives, *qua* imperatives.

This trend, largely emphasizing the view that imperatives somehow "contain" indicative statements, supports the possibility of articulating a logic of imperatives in terms of the indicatives imperatives are assumed to reflect. Work in this connection had been done by W. Dubislav, J. Jorgensen, K. Grelling, Sorainen, Hofstadter and McKinsey, and others. What is of special importance is how these men conceived of inference with respect to imperatives. Thus, as a further development of the positivists' treatment of imperatives, the work of those who adopted the general position of positivism will be considered as well.

Opposed to the above outlook, which subordinates

imperatives to indicative expressions, is the view of E.L. Beardsley. Mrs. Beardsley is the first to see that those who accept the positivistic view fail to understand the semantical function of indicatives, insofar as they predicate, and the pragmatic function of imperatives, insofar as they order. Though the distinction between the semantic and pragmatic modes of analysis is not sharply presented by Mrs. Beardsley, what is unique about her criticism is that she sees how imperatives involve the *pragmatic* relation of "ordering." Hence her observation both effectively counters the arguments of the positivists, and allows for the possibility of exploring the entire problem of imperative inference in a light free from the sharp dichotomies of positivism.

Two approaches towards the development of a logic of imperatives emerge from the above study. The first, the more prominent in recent times, assumes the imperatives are *translatable* into indicatives, which are analogous to commands. The second, briefly touched upon by Mrs. Beardsley, treats imperatives as linguistic entities distinct indicatives, and having a function different from indicatives. Furthermore, these two ways of considering imperatives reflect two modes of semantic analysis. For though Mrs. Beardsley does not outwardly say that her analysis of imperatives is extensional rather than intensional, her many references to how imperatives *designate* states of affairs indicates that her semantic analysis of imperatives is extensional. Positivists, on the other hand, look at imperatives within restricted contexts, and thus their analyses of imperatives are essential by intensional.

Section 1. The Non-assertive Aspect of Imperatives

In *Philosophy and Logical Syntax*, Carnap states that to all norms in the imperative form there corresponds value-judgments. Thus in the case of the imperative "Do not kill!" there corresponds the value-judgment : "Killing is wrong." However, insofar as a norm is in the imperative mode, it is "not...regarded as an assertion." Moreover, the value-judgment of the imperative, though like the imperative insofar as it expresses a disposition, is misleading in that it is a proposition which cannot be true or false.[25]

Carnap also presses the point that imperatives do not assert anything by pointing out that from their value-judgments nothing follows, in the sense that no propositions can be deduced from such judgments with some new knowledge being gained thereby. Hence imperatives are not publicly verifiable or inferable in a deductive system. The only way Carnap sees for imperatives to yield any new knowledge is for them to be taken in a psychological context, wherein they are considered as statements concerning an individual's character or emotional reaction. For taken in themselves, as grammatical objects open to investigation, imperatives do not assert anything. Thus he relegates them to the already enormous field of so-called metaphysical statements.[26]

It would be unfair to Carnap to say nothing concerning his views on the nature of meaning with respect to imperatives. In an earlier essay, "The Elimination of Metaphysics Through Logical Analysis," Carnap explains that a statement is *meaningful* only if it is reducible to fundamental "observational" or "protocol" sentences, which express the original sentence empirically. The latter are syntactically correct sentences, about which questions may be asked, such as what can be deduced from them, how they are logically true, how they are verified, and what they generally mean. He views such questions as dealing with the "criterion of application" which a word or sentence may be determined to have. Furthermore, these questions "ultimately" involve each other, for if something is found to be deducible from a protocol sentence then it can be determined as logically true, ostensibly verifiable, meaningful, etc.[27]

In the same essay he goes on to say that "the objective validity of a value or norm is...not empirically verifiable nor deducible from empirical statements; hence it cannot be asserted (in a meaningful statement) at all." Thus imperatives are only expressions of attitude or desire on the part of the imperator. Their observational sentences are in effect "pseudo-sentences," since, because they do not assert, no criterion of application can be considered for them. In this way, therefore, imperatives are cognitively meaningless.[28]

What Carnap denies for imperatives is that they can be translated from the material mode of speech to the formal mode of speech. In other words, because imperatives have no objectively determinable object, they cannot be rendered into a mode of speech which deals with the syntactical ('subject-predicate') form of sentences.

Moritz Achlick maintains essentially the same position as Carnap with respect to the psychological nature of norms. In his essay, "What is the Aim of Ethics?" he sees nothing detrimental to ethics if it is considered as an aspect of behavioural psychology. Taking ethics from a behaviourist viewpoint allows for solving the problem concerning the nature of the motives of human behaviour, along empiricists' lines. Hence, in this psychological reduction of ethics, there is made possible for the investigation of norms (moral imperatives) a "physicalistic" foundation which is ostensibly open to examination.[29]

Similarly, A.J. Ayer in *Language, Truth, and Logic* states that one of the classes of statements with which ethics deals with is the exhortation, which is not properly a true or false statement. Ayer states that exhortations, like ejaculations, are uttered for the purpose of arousing the hearer to action of a certain kind. As such, commands do not belong to any sector of philosophy or science. They are expressions about which no question can arise, since they reflect only the speaker's attitude about a particular situation. Also, their use lies in the way they elicit emotions in others.[30]

It is important to reflect on how the positivists' entire outlook on imperatives thus far has arisen from a general criticism of ethics. Common to Carnap, Schlick and Ayer

is the view that imperatives as *moral exhortations*, assert
nothing and are thus not propositions. These men do not
consider imperatives in the broader context of linguistic
expressions, which function differently from indicatives.
Rather they see imperatives as meaningless or noncognitive
utterances because *in ethics* they are found to express
attitudes.

Stevenson, while following the positivistic view that
imperatives express attitudes, goes one step beyond in seeking to explain how "reasons" influence imperatives. His
central thesis is that there can be no disagreement in
attitude, but there can be disagreement in belief. Thus
Stevenson holds that reasons "support" beliefs, which in
turn form attitudes. Here he goes on to distinguish between
emotive expressions which make up one aspect of moral
statements, and imperatives, which are moral statements,
"motivated by" (caused by) beliefs. In order for there to
be a change of attitude or an altering of an imperative there
must be a change in belief. However, whereas an imperative may be directly linked to the individual's belief, his
attitude is more often seen as not founded upon clearly
determinable and rational reasons.[31]

Thus Stevenson comes closest than any of the above to
attributing to imperatives a sense of rationality, and avoids
making imperatives *completely* emotive. Though he does not
go as far as to say that all imperatives are rationally traced
back to objectively determinable reasons, he does allow for
a degree of meaningfulness for imperatives *per se*, insofar
as he distinguishes them from emotive expressions *per se*.
Thus he shows how beliefs are the *foundation* of imperatives, which means that reasons or "interests" operate in
the forming of beliefs and the giving of imperatives.

In general, the position of positivism is that imperatives
per se are expressions which do not designate anything, but
which only reflect an individual's state of mind. It is seen
that imperatives have meaning insofar as they are interpreted into some indicative sentence about psychology or, in

the case of Stevenson, about an individual's beliefs. Thus imperatives are in the sense *subordinated to* or made to be *depended upon* the indicatives which express their meaning. This subordination of imperatives to indicatives is the conclusion which other linguistic analysis take from positivism, when attempting to evolve their own logic of imperatives. In this way the works of W. Dubislav, J. Jorgensen, and others presuppose the contributions of the positivists on the notion of imperatives.

The positivists' outlook on imperatives is indicative of the trend which sought to discard everything which expressed the feelings of an individual, and considered meaningful only that which is empirically verifiable. However, as is so evident with early positivism, the sharp dichotomies it draws between the meaningful and the meaningless are often untenable. In this case, it is seen that apart from their emotive quality, imperatives also have an informative content. For they order or command that something is to be done by someone. This aspect of imperatives is "meaningful." However, no translation into indicatives needs to take place so as to determine that an imperative requires that someone do something.

Furthermore, the so-called translation of imperatives into indicative statements about the imperator's state of mind seems more to distort rather than to clarify the meaning of imperatives. For example, the imperative : Shut the door ! only means that the imperator wants a certain door closed at some time. To say that such an imperative is meaningful only if one translates it in terms of the imperator's state of mind needlessly confuses the meaning of the imperative. Here positivists would object, saying that only moral imperatives are meaningless, and it is of such imperatives that the intended translation is to be performed. If this is so, then positivists must at least admit that not *all* imperatives are meaningless. However, even if their position is that only moral imperatives are meaningless, unless they are translated psychologically, they have still to give conclusive arguments for their view. For one

could always point to the case of he who says : "Do not
kill !", and maintain that this imperative arises from his
acceptance of the Ten Commandments. Certainly, if his
imperative is totally meaningless, then there would be no
way in which one could say that this imperative can be
"justified." For one could never give reasons for a
meaningless statement. Yet, the moral imperative in question can be "supported" by evidence of whether or not the
person who utters it does in fact accept the Commandments
he refers to. Moreover, no necessity arises for the translating of this imperative in terms of the imperator's mental
disposition so as to clarify it. As in the other case, to
translate the imperative : "Do not kill !" psychologically is
to confuse its meaning.

The above objections to the positivistic outlook only
underscore the evident rigidity of the sharp dichotomies
which positivists of the thirties thought in terms of. Yet it
was this line of thought which rendered imperatives *per se*
meaningless, which others adopted from positivism, in
attempting to formulate their own logic of imperatives.

Section 2. The Primacy of the Indicativeness of Imperatives

Walter Dubislav and Jorgen Jorgensen seek to develop
the positivists' view that imperatives apart from their indicative counterpart are meaningless. Their aim is to explain
how imperatives can be "translated" into indicatives. It is
this issue which now engages the efforts of most thinkers
who generally accept the positive reduction of imperatives
to indicatives.

In his article, "*Zur Ubergrunbarkeit der Forderungssatze*," Walter Dubislav maintains that to every imperative
(*Forderungssatz*) there corresponds an assertive sentence
(*Behauptungassatze*). He distinguishes between a true and
false assertion on two accounts : (1) A protocol (or observational) sentence is true if and only if it is completely in
conformity with an empirical statement which has to do
with what the protocol sentence asserts, (2) An entire
hypothesis is said to be true if, in conjunction with true

protocol sentences, there are derivable sentences with protocol characteristics (*Protokollcharakter*) which are true.[32]

Observing that ethical intuition cannot objectively determine the validity of an imperative, Dubislav states that only where the protocol sentences of imperatives are brought forth can imperatives be properly formalized, and their truth determined. He goes on to say that imperatives must thus be handled as and assumed to be observational or assertive sentences ("... *wenn man Forderungssatze wie Behauptungssatze behandelt und annimmt...*"), in either of two senses indicated above, in order for imperatives to have a *foundation* upon which their verification or falsification is objectively possible.[33]

By way of illustration, Dubislav considers the imperative : "Thou shalt not kill!" The latter is seen to be analogous to the formal statement :

'$((x) \{f(x) \supset (f(y) \supset -(xRy))\}. f(a). f(b)) \supset (-(aRb))$'.

This expression states the tautology that where 'f' is a propositional function whose value is a man; 'xRy' is a relation which says that y is killed by x ; 'a' designates Cain ; and 'b' designates Abel, and if for every x and for every y it is not the case that x kills y, then where 'a' is a man and 'b' is a (different) man, then it is not the case that a (Cain) kills b (Abel). This entire formalized expression illustrates how, when imperatives are taken of asserting logical relations, there is made possible formal inference between imperatives. In this case, that Cain must not kill Abel follows from the generalized formal expression, which expressed the imperative : "Thou shalt not kill!"[34]

Prior to considering the imperatival content of the above formula, it is important to note that Dubislav asks his reader to view imperatives as formalized assertive expressions. This is no opposition to looking at imperatives as expressions whose distinguishing characteristic is urgency and necessity of action. For Dubislav, the temporal parameter which the formal expressions he brings forth posit is assumed to be broad enough to express the imperative mood. In this way he believes he has accommodated imperatives within a two-valued deductive system. For, by translating imperatives into formal assertive propositions, then, trivially, other formal assertive propositions can be shown to formally follow from them.

However, in spite of the example given by Dubislav, it is not clear how the formula he presents illustrates the nature of imperative inference. For he has not shown how the expression : '{f (x)⊃(f (y)⊃—(xRy))}', which he takes as the formalized expression for "Thou shalt not kill!", in any way reflects that it is an imperative. At most it can be taken as an indicative statement about the way 'x' is not R-related to 'y'. Even with this interpretation one would be granting too much, since the way one is to translate the symbol '⊃' is a problem in itself. However, if one were to follow Dubislav and say that his formula illustrates imperative inference, then the formalized expression is not a statement *about* anything. It is properly an imperative, or at least must be an imperative if it is to say anything about imperative inference. Yet Dubislav says that imperatives should be looked upon as assertive expressions, in a sense which distinguishes them from imperatives of an ordinary sense. Thus Dubislav's formula presents one with a problem. On the one hand, his formula is not an imperative in the usual sense, but the formula is to tell us something about imperative reasoning, as it is ordinarily manifested. On the other hand, he wants the reader to look upon imperatives as asserted sentences, but he insists that the formula he gives tells us something about "imperative reasoning," and not about indicative inference.

Jorgen Jörgensen, while generally adopting Dubislav's position that imperative inference is akin to the inferring of indicatives, examines closely the reasons why the translating of imperatives into indicatives is the only plausible way to account for imperative inference. In "Imperatives and Logic," Jörgensen determines why imperatives, considered in the broad sense of commands, requests, appeals, wishes, etc., are in themselves not open to inference. He defines "inference" by referring to Professor Joseph's definition of "a process of thought which, starting from one or more judgments, ends in another judgment whose truth is seen to be involved in that of the former." The key word Jörgensen concentrates upon is "judgment." For, since imperatives are not judgments, imperatives can be neither premises nor conclusions in a chain of inference. In this respect also Jorgensen adopts and expands upon Poincare's early observation that because imperatives are not judgments they cannot serve in a formal syllogism.[35]

Furthermore, Jörgensen indicates that validity, as defined by Susan Stebbing, involves the distinction between "epistemic" and "constitutive" conditions of validity for an inference having premise p and consequence q. According to Stebbing, the "constitutive conditions" of validity are that p must be true, and p must imply q. On the other hand, the "epistemic conditions" of validity are that p must be known, and p must be known to imply q, without it being known that q is true.[36]

However, imperative inference is not held to be valid in any of the two sense indicated above, since no judgments are involved in such inference. Jörgensen asks his reader to consider whether "Be quiet!" can be true or false. Also, if one maintains that the latter is a judgment, he asks what the conditions of verification for such a judgment would be.[37] Jörgensen's reliance on the positivistic approach is evident here. For he requests some sort of test or "verification" by which to confirm that an imperative is true or false. Since no kind of verification accrues for imperatives, they cannot be derived from indicative premises, nor can they serve as premises from which to infer indicative conclusions. Generally, then imperatives *qua* imperatives cannot serve as any part of a logical argument.

Jörgensen goes on to say that the best means for handling imperatives inferentially is to consider the indicative "parallel-sentence" which imperatives are assumed to reflect as stated by Dubislav. Thus imperatives are seen to contain two factors : (1) the *"imperative factor,"* which indicates "something is commanded," and (2) the *"indicative factor,"* which describes "what it is that is commanded". Whereas the imperative factor is not separate from its indicative factor, since it is impossible for an imperative to have not content, the indicative factor can be taken as distinct from the imperative factor, since the latter can be formalized and other indicatives can be derived from it.[38]

In retrospect, Jörgensen points out that the phrase "is to be" (with respect to the mode of imperatives) describes "a kind of quasi-property which is ascribed to an action to be performed respecting the state of affairs to be produced." This assumption about prospected action is open to verification, and thus the formalization of imperatives is made possible:[39]

Finally, Jörgensen also recognizes that evolving a logic of imperatives as analogous to a logic of indicatives dispenses with the imperative mood. That is, the general sense of immediacy which is involved by imperatives cannot be sustained in a logic which deals with the relations between indicative sentences. However, the "content" of the imperative is not impaired; all that is lost is the information about the imperator's state of mind.[40]

Essentially, what Jörgensen is maintaining with his distinction between the imperative and indicative factors is the total abandonment of the idea that a logic of imperatives *qua* imperatives is feasible. For his claim that *only* the indicative factor of imperatives is meaningful posits the rejection of the emotive element as a part of a logic of imperatives. However, the distinction given by Jörgensen was not readily accepted by others who sought to preserve the element of immediacy within a logic of imperatives.

Commenting upon Jörgensen's differentiation between the imperative and indicative factors, Kurt Grelling attempts a different approach at developing a logic of imperatives. While staying within the general positivists' view that imperatives merely express feelings, he explores the possibility of expanding the meaning of "inference" to accommodate imperatives within a chair of inference. Underlying his view is the dissatisfaction with the thesis that the imperatives mood must be sacrificed in order for there to be a logic of imperatives. Grelling's position, therefore, is that imperatives are sentences, though *not* in the usual "logical" sense in which a sentence is said to be either true or false: "...*nicht Satze im gewohnliche Logik sein*..."[41]

By way of illustrating how imperatives are true or false, Grelling sets down the following two syllogisms :

(1) All promises are to be kept.
This is a promise.

Therefore : This (promise) is to be kept,

(2) Your love of your neighbour is to be equal to your love of yourself.

You are to love yourself.

Therefore : You are to love your neighbour."

In 1) the first premiss is an imperative, which forms part of the syllogism, and is schematized by Grelling as "from 'x' and 'y' there follows 'z'". However, the first premiss being an imperative, the schema of syllogism is altered by him to "from 'that 'x' ought to be' and 'y' there follows 'that 'z' ought to be true.'" So as to allow the conclusion to follow logically from the premisses, Grelling finds it necessary to set down the following rule : "if 'x' and 'y' 'z' follows, then from the conjunction of 'that 'x' ought to be' and 'y' it follows 'that 'z' ought to be true.'" Thus Grelling believes he has expanded the meaning of logical implication sufficiently so as to include imperatives *qua* imperatives into formal logical reasoning. The rule given is supposed to illustrate an assumed "logical implication" for inference where imperatives are involved. Grelling gives another rule to cover his second syllogism to the effect that : "If it follows from 'x' 'that 'y' ought to be true,' then it is implied by "x' ought to be true,' that 'y' ought to be true." Like the former, this rule is supposed to illustrate an assumed logical implication.[42]

Grelling's departure from Jörgensen is in the way he tries to steer away from the alternative of subordinating imperatives to the indicatives they are said to reflect, and tries to develop a logic of imperatives which preserves the imperative mood, and yet makes inference possible. The rules he gives are thus said to reflect the general syntax of of imperative sentences."[43]

The approach presented by Grelling is in turn strongly attacked by K. Reach, who subscribes to Jörgensen's approach of subordinating imperatives to indicatives. According to Reach, Grelling's basic notion that imperatives are sentences, though, not in *usual* sense of the term, is obscure. For Grelling states that he considers imperatives as "*Annahmen*" or assumptions. Yet Reach points out that assumptions ordinarily can be taken to be true or false, in which case Grelling's presentation is unclear. Furthermore, Reach states that Grelling's first rule is false. For, if 'z' is substituted for 'x', and 'non-z' for 'y', then there results : "The conjunction of 'z' and 'that non-z ought to be true' implies that 'z' ought to be true." This result, though consistent, renders Grelling's expansion of the notion of logical implication useless. For Grelling is saying by the above that the conjunction of two contrary things (z and non z) implies one of the conjuncts. Reach points out that this is absurd, since Grelling's sense of implication allows that from a false expression (the above conjunction) something true (i.e. z) can follow. In order for the notion of implication to have any useful function it must state that nothing follows from a false expression; i.e. neither true nor false statements may follow from false statements. As it turns out, Grelling must go on and say that it also follows from his conjunction that non-z ought to be true as well. Herein lies the absurdity of Grelling's conception of implication, as regards imperatives.[44]

Another attack upon the position of Dubislav and Jorgensen is that by Grue-Sorensen, who believes that logical validity (of a sort) is applicable to syllogisms containing imperatives. Grue Sorensen's central argument is that syllogisms containing imperatives either in the premisses or in the conclusion, or both, do not have the usual logical validity of syllogisms, but rather have "logoid" (*logoiden*) values, which are moral conditions of validity or invalidity. It is important to bear in mind that Grue-Sorensen is referring only to moral imperatives and by validity he has in mind a kind of moral propriety and obligation. More importantly, his argument is aimed at dislodging Jorgensen's sweeping claim that *no* imperative is ever true or false, since no imperative is empirically verifiable. For ethical imperatives are distinguishable for non-ethical imperatives, in Grue-Sorensen's view. The uniqueness of ethical imperatives is that once one is uttered, for example, "Do unto others as you would have others do unto you!", then the imperative : "Treat (person) X fairly!" follows from the preceding imperative (together with such premisses as : "To treat X fairly is doing unto someone as you (the person addresses) would have others do unto you (the person addressed)!") with a validity that arises from the very *meaning* and *acceptance* of the first premiss in conjunction with the second premiss.[45]

In so considering ethical imperatives, Grue-Sorensen hopes to base ethics on a scientific (deductive) foundation. In this respect he seeks to counter both Jörgensen's denial that such a foundation for ethics is possible, and Poincare's early observation that morality cannot be considered as a deductive science.

The thrust of Grue-Sorensen's attack is thus that "moral" imperatives are meaningful and have a rationality which is distinct from that of indicatives. His attack upon Jörgensen differs from that of Grelling's therefore, in that Grue-Sorensen does not say that all imperatives are meaningless, nor does he tamper with two-valued logic to accommodate imperatives. In so far as Grue-Sorensen seeks the rationality of imperatives within the meaning of imperatives themselves, his approach is similar to that of Ernst

Mally's. Yet insofar as he sees a problem arising in relating indicatives and imperatives, Grue-Sorensen's approach to the issue of developing a calculus of imperatives is linguistically more sensitive than Mally's.

Kalle Sorainen's objection to Jörgensen's distinction between imperative and indicative factors is the last important criticism of Jörgensen's view. Sorainen objects to Jörgensen's distinction on the grounds that the difference between imperatives and indicatives is modal rather than logical, and thus the "sharp" distinction between the two modes of expression have no logical support. He points out that modal difference is explained only in terms of psychological reasons, and the latter does not harbour any clear-cut distinction between imperatives and indicatives : *"Psychologisher lasst sichdiese scharfe Distinktion such nicht vertieidigen...."*[46]

It is important to realize that Sorainen does not deny that imperatives have an indicative meaning; rather he objects to Jörgensen's subordinating of imperatives to indicatives. Sorainen believes that the psychological interpretation of imperatives reveals that the context in which imperatives are uttered has an indicative dimension. According to Sorainen, it is the psychological context of imperatives which illustrates that the indicative factor of imperatives cannot function alone, and that in order for imperatives to be true or false in a two-valued propositional calculus they must be considered in the way they reflect the imperator's state of mind, and the general psychological context in which imperatives are uttered. For these reasons, Sorainen rejects the view that the imperative and indicative factor of imperatives are completely separate, and that the former is meaningful while the latter is not.

Thus Jörgensen's distinction between an indicative and an imperative factor introduces into the problem of formulating a logic of imperatives the issue of translating imperatives into indicatives. Indeed, much of the criticism which arose soon after Jörgensen published his article centres on the very issue of whether one needs to perform the aforementioned translation, as Grelling's, Grue-Sorensen's and Sorainen's commentaries illustrate. In this connection, the work of Hofstadter and McKinsey proceeds one step beyond the contribution of Jörgensen. For, by assuming that imperatives are analogous to declaratives, and that the latter insofar as they are renderable in a two-valued logic, are the ultimate basis for a logic of imperatives, these men become the first to attempt a calculus of imperatives within the Carnapian formal language LI. It is to this attempt that attention is now turned, after which criticism of those who assert the indicatival basis for imperatives will be given.

Hofstadter and McKinsey begin by distinguishing between two kinds of imperatives, "fiats" and "directives." The latter are taken as imperatives where the agent is specifically identified, whereas in the former there is no such reference. Furthermore, they distinguish between the *"satisfaction"* of an imperative and its *"correctness."* Accordingly, an imperative is satisfied if that which is commanded "is the case." On the other hand, an imperative is said to be correct if what is commanded "ought" or "ought not" to be the case.[47]

For Hofstadter and McKinsey the above definitions make possible the extension of Carnap's language LI, with certain additions to its primitives. The result hoped for is a *"combined"* formal language of indicatives and imperatives. The new language, Ic, has, in addition to the primitives and postulates of LI in *The Logical Syntax of Language*, the following primitives :

'!', '—', '+', '=', '×', '→', and '>'.[48]

To clarify their use one must consider Carnap's language LI. In the introduction to *The Logical Syntax of Language*, Carnap states that his objective is to show how the logical characteristics of sentences are completely dependent upon the *syntactical structure* of sentences. Thus by expanding the usual sense of "syntax," and formulating it with some exactitude, one will be able to include the study of logic

within an examination of syntax. Thus Carnap suggests
that the logical rules of deduction (or *transformation rules*)
can be formulated in syntactical terms. The resulting syntax
is termed the "logical syntax" of a language. However, it
is not the logical syntax of ordinary language which Carnap
sets out to develop, but the logical syntax of constructed
symbolic languages. For the development of the former is
not practical, since words of this language have no one fixed
meaning. Hence the system of simple and rigid rules,
which will enable him to show the characteristics and range
of application of logical syntax, is what Carnap terms
"language I" or LI.[49]

Hofstadter and McKinsey proceed to augment LI, by
adopting certain operators. They say that the primitive '!'
introduces the uniary operator "let it be the case that...,"
which is derived from the sentence say "The place 3 is
blue." It is essential to their attempt that imperatives are
derived from (*"made from"*) indicative sentences, since they
articulate their logic of imperative as *analogous* to a logic of
indicatives.[50]

Hofstadter and McKinsey point out that the opposite or
contrary of an imperative will be introduced by the symbol
'—', which, placed over the command designated by 'C,'
indicates that this command is not satisfied. The symbol '+'
serves the same purpose of 'v' (alternation) in the propositional calculus, when taken in an inclusive sense. Thus
where 'C_1' is the imperative "Let the place 3 be blue!" and
'C_2' is the imperative "Let the place 4 be red", the expression 'C_1—C_2' states "Either let the place 3 be blue or let the
place 4 be red (inclusively)."[51]

The conjunction of imperative is expressed by '×', where
'$C_1 \times C_2$' express the command "let the place 3 be blue and
let the place 4 be red." This expression is satisfied when 'C_1'
and 'C_2' are *both* satisfied. Also, the symbol '→' expresses
implication in the following way : '$S_1 \to C_2$' means that if 'S_1'
designates the sentence "The place 2 is blue", then "Let the
place 3 be blue!" is to be satisfied. The entire expression,
'$S_1 \to C_2$' is satisfied if 'S_1' is false or 'C_1' is satisfied. How-

ever, if 'S_1' is false than 'C_1' does not have to be performed, but if 'C_1' is performed, then it does not matter whether or not 'S_1' is true.

Whereas the above five symbols are explained in terms of imperatives which yield expressions that are imperatives, the symbol '$>$' constructs sentences out of imperatives. This symbol expresses material inclusion, and is analogous to material implication in the two-valued propositional logic. Thus given 'C_1' and 'C_2', the expression '$C_1 > C_2$' is the sentence "Let the place 3 be blue; includes let the place 4 be red."[53]

Some symbols from Carnap's language I are retained by Hofstadter and McKinsey. For example, '$=$', which expresses equivalence between numbers and sentences in LI, is used by them to indicate material equality between imperatives. Thus '$C_1 = C_2$' states "Let the place 3 be blue, equals let the place 4 be red." The latter is true when the sentence "'If the place 3 is blue, then the place 4 is red, and if the place 4 is red. then the placc 3 is blue." is true.[54]

Universal and existential operators are defined as follows. In the case of the former, the universal quantifier is placed before the imperative such that if 'C_1' is the imperative "Let the nth place be blue!" then '$(n)7(C_1)$' expresses the imperative "For every $n > 7$, let the nth place be blue!" On the other hand, the existential operator in front of the imperative results in an expression such that '$(\exists n)7(C_1)$' reads "For some $n > 7$, let the nth place be blue!"[55]

Hofstadter and McKinsey claim that all syntactical designations of Carnap's language Ll are retained in Ic, as well as the symbols : 'C_1', 'C_2,' '...' for imperatives, and all other symbols discussed above. Furthermore, every sentence of Ll is a numerical expression of Ic. In addition, Ic contains rules of formation, following and including those of language Ll. Examples of primitive sentences of Ic, in addition to those of Ll, are :

PSI 12. '$\bar{S}_1 = ! - S_1$',

......

PSI 16. '$(!S_1 > !S_2) \equiv (S_1 \supset S_2)$',

......

PSI 22. '$(C_1 = C_2) \supset (\bar{C}_1 = \bar{C}_2)$',

56

......

Extending the general procedure of employing the various aspects of Ll in Ic, they state that if 'S_1' is a 'provable' sentence in Ll, it is also 'provable' in Ic; the same holds for 'S_1' being "refutable," "irresoluble," "analytic," "contradictory," "synthetic," and "consequence of" in Ll.[57]

The authors proceed to give the first theorem of Ic as that all imperative-connectives, except the symbol : '!', can be eliminated from indicatives, as well as from imperatives. Thus it can *be* proven that '$C_1 = !S_1$' is provable, making 'S_1' in turn derivable within Ic. Hence it can be shown that 'C_1' is "provable," "refutable," "irresoluble," etc. Also, if it can be shown that '$C_1 = !S_1$' and that '$C_2 = !S_2$' are provable, then 'C_2' is derivable from 'C_1', if 'S_2' is derivable from 'S_1'. In similar ways, Hofstadter and McKinsey go on to define the "*equipollence*" of 'C_1' and 'C_2', as well as other syntactical concepts which are applicable to both sentences and imperatives.[58]

The entire attempt offered by Hofstadter and McKinsey is founded upon the idea that imperatives are "made out of" sentences. Thus the articulation of a logic of imperatives as analogous to a sentential logic, such as the one offered by Carnap, seems entirely justified. The authors explicitly state that they do not treat imperatives as declaratives, but as distinct from declaratives. Furthermore, they find nothing wrong with the reduction of the symbol '!' to superfluity because of the equipolence of every imperative to some non-imperative sequence. The latter follows trivially from the very approach which Hofstadter and McKinsey adopt, as was seen in the presentation of their attempt. In effect they find it desirable to be able to introduce '!' anywhere in a language, and thus prove a theorem in that language as a theorem of imperative logic.[59]

Thus Hofstadter and McKinsey present an imperative logic, which, though seeking to preserve the imperative mood of imperatives, treats imperatives as somehow derived from declarative sentences, *though* apparently distinct from declaratives. The ambivalence of this outlook reflects the problem of relating imperatives to declaratives, going back to Jörgensen and his adaptation of the positivists' position that imperatives apart from indicatives are meaningless. Certainly the ambivalence of Hofstadter and McKinsey's view on the relation of the calculus of imperatives to the sentential calculus Carnap's language I results from obscurity as to how imperatives are dependent upon or, as they say, "made from" indicative sentences, which is first manifest in Carnap's view that imperatives are meaningful only if they are taken as psychological statements.

A criticism of Hofstadter and McKinsey thus involves a criticism of all who generally adopt the positivists' reduction of imperatives. In view of this, a thorough discussion of the views of E.A. Beardsley is appropriate. For she analyzes the entire movement from Jörgensen and Dubislav to Hofstadter and McKinsey, which is permeated with the issue involving the relation between imperatives and indicatives.

Section 3. Beardsley's Differentiation Between the Semantical Function of Imperatives and Indicatives

Elizabeth Beardsley concentrates upon the way the imperators intend his imperative to function. Hence she departs from the above views, which deal with how imperatives relate to what they connote psychologically. From Beardsley's position, imperatives are seen as distinct linguistic entities, having a meaning independent of indicatives, which arises from the very use imperatives are determined to have in language. The importance of her study is that it brings about a cleavage in the analyses of imperatives, which is basically that of the intensional mode of analysis, and the extensional and pragmatic mode of analysis. The former, introduced by Dubislav and Jörgensen, undergoes refinements by Alf Ross and others. The latter mode of analysis, though not sharply delineated by Mrs Beardsley, also undergoes some refinement. However, followers of this latter view are few.[60]

Beardsley points out in "Imperative Sentences in Relation to Indicatives," the evident trend of writers to treat imperatives as somehow *subordinate* to indicatives. She finds this outlook unacceptable, because it fails to preserve the distinctive features of imperatives. Therefore, she endeavours to explore the grounds for maintaining that imperatives are "coordinated with, rather than subordinated to indicatives."[61]

However, before going on with Mrs Beardsley's discussion it is important to consider what she has to say, in an earlier essay, about the proper characterizations of sentences. For her views in "The Semantical Aspect of Sentences" explicate how the syntactical analysis of sentences relates to their semantic analysis. This becomes important for understanding in the later essay what she means by a sentence, used by an individual to bring about a certain action.[62]

Consequently, she states that a sentence, while it is a group of words, is something more than the sum of its parts. Sentences differ from merely a group of unrelated words, or from a number of words constituting a phrase. Furthermore, sentences cannot be characterized solely on a syntactical level, as a sequence of words containing a subject and a predicate with modifiers, and expressing a complete thought. Beardsley points out that the very notions of "subject" and "predicate" can only be defined semantically, though they appear in a syntactical language. Thus, for Beardsley, there is no sharp distinction between the syntactical and the semantical characterization of a sentence. Any explanation of the syntactical order of words must touch upon some aspect of the semantical features of such words. Thus when one speaks of the syntactical relation of the subject to the predicate, for example, one is assuming that there is already defined in a precise manner all that constitutes a "subject", and what constitutes a "predicate."[63]

All syntactical descriptions, therefore, have some semantical overtones, in so far as such descriptions have a role to play in ordinary discourse. Conversely, one cannot speak of the meaning of an expression without also making some assumptions about its syntax. For to speak of the meaning of this or that expression means that one has already decided on what is to count for a complete expression. In this way syntactics is involved in semantics.[64]

In her later essay, Beardsley goes on to say that the term 'sentence' cannot be defined apart from its syntactical *and* semantical characteristics. Thus the meaningful characteristics of indicative sentences is that they "predicate" the events or state of affairs they deal with. It is thus the semantical function of indicatives, whether in the object-language or in the syntax-language, to predicate the existence or occurrence of some state of affairs. As *distinct from* the semantic function of indicatives, Beardsley points to the "pragmatic relation" involved in "assertion." The latter is taken as the relation between an indicative sentence and the user of that sentence.[65]

It is important to clearly state her view on the nature of commands, for it is the basis from which she attacks other views. Hence it is emphasized that Mrs Beardsley sees imperatives as sentences which are *employed* for bringing about something. This "performative" function of imperatives is distinct from the function of indicatives. In the latter case, one has statements which only state or describe *that* such and such is the case.

It is the failure to recognize the distinction between the linguistic function of indicatives and imperatives that has led to the incorrect conclusion that imperatives are translatable into indicatives. For this reason Jörgensen's attempt suffers, since it fails to explain how the psychological aspect of an imperative (taken as *either* an indicative or an imperative) can convey something about the imperator's attitude, and still be the grounds for saying that imperatives are meaningless. For in that Jörgensen holds that imperatives do not in themselves express any fact, they cannot say anything about the speaker's attitude. Yet, on the other hand, imperatives *per se* are said to be assertions about the imperator's attitude. Hence they are not meaningless, and they can be said to be, in some (pragmatic) sense, true or false. Jorgensen, however, never stops to consider how imperatives are to be considered, that is as either indicatives or commands. For this reason there is a certain vagueness as to how imperatives can say anything about the imperator's attitude.[66]

Furthermore, Beardsley defines "attitude" as the desire on the part of the imperator to have his command satisfied. In her view, one can infer the imperative attitude from the *form* of the imperative. This desire on the part of the imperator is the "pragmatic ground" for considering the imperative as a distinct linguistic form. It is the imperator's desire which determines the way in which the indicative sentence is used to effect the desired action. Thus the resulting expression (the imperative) is the product of the imperator's intention or desire, which Beardsley terms the "pragmatical implicate." On the whole, Jörgensen's error is that he completely neglects the nature of the relation between this "pragmatic implicate" and the imperative itself.[67]

Thus it is the "ordering" or assertive aspect of imperatives, which for Beardsley makes the introduction of an indicative factor to account for the meaningfulness and truth of imperatives unnecessary. For imperatives are meaningful because they assert the speaker's desires, and they are also true in the pragmatic sense of something being or not being asserted by someone.

However rough Mrs Beardsley's views may be, it is interesting to see how they may extend to the earlier positivists' reduction of imperatives. For in light of her views, the positivists' treatment of imperatives is seen to be incomplete. The psychological statement which, for Carnap, forms the only meaningful basis of imperatives does not take into account the assertive aspect of imperatives. Early in her article Beardsley brings out that although imperatives express a psychological attitude, it is true that indicatives express attitudes as well; thus it is not sufficient to distinguish between imperatives and indicatives on the basis that one expresses emotions while the other does not.[68]

Though Beardsley's pragmatic approach to the study of imperatives avoids some issues which the positivists' distinction between the meaningful and meaningless involve, there are nonetheless many problems in her view as well. For example, she often confuses the semantic level of linguistic analysis with the pragmatic level, and speaks of the assertive aspect of imperatives as a "semantical function" of a sentence.[69] Though as Colin Cherry points out in "*On Human Communication*," there is no clear cut demarcation between the syntactical, semantical, and pragmatic modes of linguistic analysis, this is still no reason to carelessly neglect that there are such distinctions, which, where possible, should be preserved.[70] Moreover, she does not bring out how by her saying that imperatives *designate* intentions and desires that this constitutes a *complete* extensional analysis of imperatives. Had she brought this out, it would be easier to grasp how her approach departs from those she opposes. In this respect it should also be kept in mind that the intensionalists' approach to imperatives is not exhausted by the contributions of Dubislav and the others thus far considered. As the subsequent chapters will illustrate, the intensionalists' view undergoes many refinements. Hence it is proper to look at Beardsley's view as an "alternative" to, rather than as a complete rebuttal of, the intensionalists' viewpoint.

Beardsley proceeds to review the position of Grue-Sorensen. She objects to his view that moral imperatives have a sense of validity which is absent from all other non-moral imperatives. She points out that Grue-Sorensen's argument is essentially a *petitio principii*. For the acceptance of an imperative as valid or invalid accrues for all kinds of

imperatives. Here she defines "acceptance" as the ability
of the agent to do whatever the imperator demands of him.
Evidently, however, Grue-Sorensen means that moral
imperatives have a special sense in which they are taken as
valid or invalid. Beardsley points out that somewhere along
the line Grue-Sorensen must explain that *this*, as opposed to
that, is ethically proper or improper. Thus it is seen that he
must stipulate that because he considers such-and-such to
be "ethical", this or that moral imperative can be "validly"
inferred. In this way a statement about Grue-Sorensen's
moral outlook explains why some imperative inference is
valid. Beardsley also points out that Grue-Sorensen's interpretation of imperative validity does not effect the pragmatic distinction she presents concerning the function of
indicatives and imperatives. For the latter observation is
not based on semantical considerations, as is Grue-Sorensen's definition of imperative validity, but rather deals with
language and its users, and thus involves pragmatic considerations.[71]

Beardsley also rejects Hofstadter and McKinsey's attempt
on the grounds that it does not sufficiently explain how
imperatives are "made out" of sentences, or how imperatives can "function" as sentences. Their contention that
"let it be the case that," which is designated by '!', is true
only if the expression following "it is the case that" is true,
is ambiguous. For what constitutes the truth of what follows
after "! it is the case that" does not explain "truth" for
imperatives. Surely a statement about the truth of a sentence beginning with "it is the case that" concerns the
object-language, where the subject at issue is that which is
said to be the case. To hold the sentence about the truth
of the sentence prefixed by the phrase "let it be the case
that" is equivalent to the command which is considered by
the latter, is to say that there is no distinction between the
syntax-language and the object-language. Furthermore, if
it said that the expression "Let the place 3 be blue !" is only
another way of saying "The place 3 is blue", then according
to Beardsley, the imperative mood of the command is lost.[72]

Apart from her criticism of those who sought to subordinate imperatives to indicatives, Beardsley's positive contribution is that imperatives should be looked upon as coordinated with, though distinct from, indicatives. She maintains that the above criticism enables her to show how two sentences, of different moods, can be said to have the same content, though retaining the mood of each sentence involved. For once the nature of imperatives is seen to be assertive rather than predicative, and that basically imperatives *order*, then the coordinate indicative sentence of an imperative is one which says that the action ordered by the imperative is performed. The latter, the "indicative correlate", is further explained by the following example. The indicative correlate of "Shut the door at time t!" is "You shut the door at time t." In essence, these two different semantical functions relate to the same event, which it expresses as "your shutting the door at time t." In the case of the imperative this event is ordered, whereas in the case of the indicative this event is predicated.[73]

One must not assume that Beardsley is equating imperatives and indicatives in the sense that one can be substituted for another. Her saying that imperatives are *coordinated* with indicatives aims mainly at showing the way in which the action ordered by the imperative can be expressed as directed to someone by an imperator in an indicative sense. This does not mean, however, that imperatives and indicatives are interchangeable. If one were to maintain that they are interchangeable, or that at least imperatives are replaceable by indicatives, then one would have to grant that a sentence, whether an imperative or an indicative, has more than one linguistic function, in that it can both predicate and command. This, however, is unacceptable, since a sentence can have only *one* such function in Beardsley's view.[74]

As indicated, Beardsley's criticism of the intensionalists by no means ends the efforts at arriving at a logic of imperatives by means of contextualist analyses. Also, it has been shown that Beardsley's own extensionalist and pragmatic analysis of imperatives is in turn beset with ambiguities. Thus both these ways of investigating the issue at hand should be viewed as two "distinct" alternatives, which aim for the same results, that is, a logic of imperatives. As the subsequent developments will show, the more popular intensionalists' approach will ultimately come to involve a substantial degree of complexity, while Beardsley's extensionalist analysis of imperatives provides a simpler yet unnoticed dimension as to how the problem of developing a logic of imperatives evolves in contemporary thought.

3

The Inadequacy of the Positivist' Reduction of Imperatives

The view regarding imperatives as analogous to indicatives is pursued by some in a modified form. What takes place in the study of imperatives after the above contributions is a gradual retreat from the position which categorically reduces imperatives to statements about the speaker's sentiments or state of mind. Consequently, a shift occurs away from seeing a logic of imperatives as possible only because imperatives can be translated into indicatives. This transition takes place through the careful analysis of imperatives within their connotation, and what it means to say that imperatives can be included within a formal inference.

Thus, apart from Beardsley's attack upon Dubislav and his followers, those who were to oppose the positivist reduction of imperatives proceed by means of a more penetrating intensionalist' analysis of imperatives. That is, they seek to clarify further the view that imperatives are inferable from other imperatives by looking into what is commonly accepted as connoting an imperative, and a logical inference in general.

The arguments which precipitate this shift center mainly on the question of how inference is possible with respect to imperatives. The scope of this chapter is thus to explicate this problem in the contributions of Alf Ross, H.G. Bohnert,

R.M. Hare, and others. Part of the difficulty of this task, is however, to describe the above transition, while also illustrating the continuance of the view that a logic of imperatives is possible through an intensional analysis of imperatives. Methodologically, one has with the shift from the orthodox positivist' view a refinement of the general intensional approach. For there now appears a deeper analysis *within* the trend of intensionally analyzing imperatives, initiated by earlier thinkers.

The upshot of these discussions is that there results a greater complexity as to the meaning of imperatives than is manifest in the earlier intensional analyses. The significance of this outcome is that it contradicts the stated aim of those who depart from the positivists, since they sought to *overcome* the complexity of the previous analyses. In a sense, what follows illustrates an essential fault of the intensional view, namely its cumbersome complexity. This shortcoming will be further realized as more views are reviewed in the course of this historical study of the issue. The immediate aim of the present chapter, however, is to illustrate how the shift from the early positivists takes place, and how the resulting views penetrate deeper into the *meaning* of imperatives.

Section 1.   Is Logical Inference Meaningful With Respect to the Positivist' Treatment of Imperatives ?

In "Imperatives and Logic," Alf Ross re-evaluates the view which reduces imperatives to declaratives. His main concern is to show that there is a practical ground for the immediately evident nature of imperative inference. Thus one need not avoid the sense of immediacy which imperatives exhibit when inferred, as is the practice of positivists. In this way, therefore, Ross departs from his predecessors.[75]

Ross begins by examining the meaning of the following sentence : " 'Can an imperative be a constituent part of a logical inference ?' " He defines "logical inference" as a movement of thought, beginning with one or more propositions and ending with a new proposition, whose truth is involved in the preceeding propositions. Also, "constituent part of" means that which is either the premiss or conclusion of the movement of thought indicated above. Finally, he defined an "imperative" as "a sentence, the object of which is to express an immediate demand for action, but not to describe a fact."[76]

At the very outset, however, there is a certain vagueness concerning one of Ross' central ideas. For what does it mean to say that 'inference' is a "movement of thought ?" Ross cannot mean that inference is just a psychological process, since he lays stress on the fact that propositions *form* the premisses and *involve* the conclusion of an inference. Yet, he seems to lay emphasis on the idea that inference *is* a movement of thought. Furthermore, how is one to conceive of a "movement of thought ?" Here again there is a difficulty in how one is to handle this idea. Does Ross mean by "movement" a reflection upon premisses, or does he have an "intuitive" notion of "movement" in mind ?

Ross articulates his position on the basis of the dilemma which Jörgensen sought to deal with. This dilemma results from the fact that for a sentence to be inferred from another sentence or group of sentences, the former sentence must be either true or false. However, imperatives can be neither true nor false. On the other hand, in examples such as :

> "Keep your promises.
>
> This is a promise of yours.
> _____
> Keep this promise..........."

there is *felt* that the conclusion "logically" (in an unspecified sense) follows from the premisses. Hence arises the dilemma of the above two aspects of imperatives. As stated in the presentation of Jörgensen's position, the solution of this dilemma involves the reduction of imperatives into indicatives, and then separating out the imperative factor from the indicative factors.[77]

Ross objects to Jörgensen's solution on the grounds that it does not explain what it means to say that an imperative is *inferred* from corresponding sentences. Schematically, he presents the issue as follows :

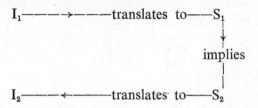

The real problem is to explain what it means to infer imperative I_2 from imperative I_1. This issue is different from that of *how* I_1 can be translated into sentences S_1, and from S_1 to arrive at (to infer) S_2, which is a translation of I_2. The rules for these translations do not explain what it means to infer I_2 from I_1. They only state how an imperative may be rendered in the indicative mood. What Ross questions is the meaning of such an inference, since Ross defines "inference" as a "movement of thought" from a number of propositions (in Ross' sense) to a new proposition which is the conclusion and which is involved by the preceding propositions. To explain the translating "procedure" going from I_1 to I_2 does not explain what the meaning of such an inference (I_2 from I_1) is. Thus the dilemma Jörgensen attempts to solve remains.[78]

One solution to the above dilemma, entertained by most previous writers, is that the supposed inference which seems to take place when deriving I_2 from I_1 is really a pseudo-inference. Hence the only actual evidence for such an inference is a "certain feeling of evidence." Those who hold this view, e.g. J. Jörgensen, support it by saying that truth-values cannot be applied to imperatives, thus there can be no such inference wherein imperatives *qua* imperatives may be inferred from imperatives *qua* imperatives. Ross observes, however, that the idea of "inference" is not attached to the values of truth or falsity, but rather to specified deductive rules. Hence Jörgensen, and others are wrong where they dismiss the possibility of developing a logic of imperatives *qua* imperatives on the basis of the fact that imperatives can be neither true nor false. For it may still be possible to infer one imperative from another, being that validity deals with formal rules of deduction, and not with truth or falsity.[79]

Ross points out that one could proceed to show that validity and invalidity are somehow analogous to the values of truth and falsity. However, to so pursue the issue leads to a still greater difficulty. For one can always define 'validity' as an agreement with certain facts. Thus ostensive verification would then determine validity, and not the conditions for formal validity, that is, validity according to the generally accepted rules of framing arguments and arriving at conclusions. Hence, imperatives could not be inferred from other imperatives, since there could never be any verification of imperative sentences.[80]

Before presenting Ross' own solution to the above dilemma, it is helpful to recapitulate his objection to the positivist solution. In essence, it consists in reminding the reader that according to the generally accepted meaning of 'inference,' there is a difference between inferring indicative conclusions from indicative premises, and inferring imperatives as conclusion from premises which are imperatives. The basis for this difference lies not in the inapplicability of true or false truth-values to imperatives, and their applicability to indicatives. Rather, imperatives are not open to inference in the same way that ordinary indicatives are, because the formal rules for validity are not applicable to imperatives, whereas they are applicable to indicatives. Hence, Jörgensen and others do not explain how imperatives are not open to inference by showing that one cannot attach truth-values to imperatives. Ross' objection is simply that validity alone determines whether something can be legitimately inferred from something else. Thus in their analyses of imperatives, those who have followed the positivist reduction of imperatives have failed to ask what it means for imperatives to be valid, in that they may be inferred from other imperatives.

Ross' own solution to the dilemma concentrates upon explaining what constitutes the "feeling" that something has been inferred, where one arives at "Keep this promise." from "Keep your promises" and "This is your promise." In his view this feeling is accountable by presenting a "logic of validity" for imperatives, *and* a "logic of satisfaction" for imperatives. It is the combination of these two logics which shows that inference with respect to imperatives is based on *Practical* considerations, and should be properly termed "logical" inference.

The author defines 'validity' for imperatives as the possession of a psychological "state of demand" by the imperator, or the possession of the psychological "state of acceptance" by the person who acts upon the imperative. 'Invalidity' would therefore be the nonpossession of these states by the respective individuals. Hence the corresponding S sentence of imperatives, will also express something about these psychological states.[82]

Yet, what is this "state of demand" or "state of acceptance" possessed by the imperator or agent of an imperative ? Ross only says that these are psychological states accompanying the giving of or the acting upon imperatives. Their possession in some way accounts for the validity of an inferred imperatives. At first glance it is evident that Ross, unlike the positivists, does not view the emotive element of imperatives as the basis for holding that imperative are meaningless. For he considers the psychological states precluded by imperatives as explicating how imperatives are valid. Yet the question remains as to how these mental states can account for validity, which, in the usual formal sense, is a notion covering the proper relations of statement in an argument. Furthermore, Ross appears to be basing imperative validity on highly tentative grounds. For one person's state of demanding differs from another's. Thus it is difficult to see how such validity can be supported.

However, Ross proceeds to distinguish between the possession of the above states, and the *theme* of the imperative. For example, one can speak in terms of the negation of the psychological state which the imperative connotes, or in terms of the negation of the content or theme of the imperative. Moreover, an imperative may be negated with respect to its content (it is not acted upon), though the imperator possesses the psychological state of demanding. Thus Ross claims that apart from the logic of imperative validity one should also give an account of the logic of the satisfaction of imperatives. In this way the complete logic of imperatives will be accounted for, and that "feeling" which accompanies imperative inference will by explicated. For it is the immediately evident nature of imperative inference which has eluded the understanding of previous thinkers.[83]

Ross attempts to meet this difficulty by proving the following hypothesis :

"That the characteristic feature of the existing practical inferences is that they purport to bring about a combination of the results to which the logic of satisfaction and the logic of validity may lead respectively...."

In the case of imperatives, this "combination" is brought out when the logic of satisfaction and the logic of validity are considered with respect to the value function of negation. For this reason mainly, consideration of the other truth-values of this combination will be deferred.[84]

With regard to the logic of satisfaction, negation occurs as follows : if the expression 'I (x)' stands for "you are to close the door," then the negation of this expression : 'I $(\bar{x})$' is "you are (not to close the door)." Trivially, if 'I $(\bar{x})$' is satisfied, then 'I $(\bar{x})$' cannot be satisfied.[85]

On the other hand, the value of negation with respect to the logic of validity is different from negation with respect to the logic of satisfaction. In the former case 'I (x)' becomes invalid when one commands or asserts "you (are not to) close the door," that is, '$\bar{I}$(x). Thus also, if 'I (x)' is valid, that is, the imperator possesses the psychological state of demand discussed above, then $\bar{I}(x)$ is invalid; the imperator does not have the state of demand, and conversely.[86]

The value function of negation, which pertains to the combination of the logic of satisfaction and the logic of validity, is the basis for the "practical inference" imperatives are found to involve. This negation, expressed as ' $I(\bar{x})$ ', means that where N commands 'I (x)', then the expression 'I (x) ' is "*non-valid.*" Here it is important to note that the inference "that 'I $(\bar{x})$ ' is "*non-valid*" if 'I (x)' is valid" constitutes, for Ross, a "reality sentence." For what this inference says is only that if someone commands that something be done, then the agent cannot simultaneously also do the opposite of what is commanded of him. This impossibility in acting in two opposing ways results not from logical considerations, but from practical modes of behaving. Thus the inference from 'I (x)' being valid to 'I $(\bar{x})$ ' being "*non-valid*" is a pseudo-logical inference. For it is possible only if there are no commands demanding some contradictory action, and this is not a *logical reason* for the validity of an inference. Ross goes on to say that in so-called imperative reasoning one assumes, as a "practical attitude of mind," that the *immediate evidence* of the above pseudo-inference warrants its acceptance as a "logical inference." However, Jörgensen and others do not logically infer "Keep this promise" from "Keep your promises" and "This is your promise," but rather follow the *practical* consequence of accepting the last two statements as true, that is, as being satisfied.[87]

In spite of Ross' subtle differentiation between the logic of imperative validity and the logic of imperative satisfaction, there is an inescapable flaw in his account of imperative inference. For he really has no grounds for calling the conclusions derived from imperative premises "imperatives." According to Ross, an imperative must be commanded by an imperator, in order for it to express the state of commanding experienced by the imperator. However, the conclusion drawn in an imperative inference is arrived at by the agent, to whom the imperative premisses are directed. Thus the conclusion cannot be valid in Ross' own sense of a statement which expresses the imperator's state of demanding. Hence no imperative conclusion, in that it is not asserted by an imperator, can ever be an imperative. Thus imperative inference, is not possible on Ross' own terms.

Furthermore, one must be careful in allowing Ross' contention that an individual's incapacity to act in two opposing ways at the same time is always due to a "practical" impossibility. For it often happens that what is practically possible or impossible at one time may not be so at another time. Thus there is a definite relativism in saying that "practical considerations" operate in determining imperative inference.

In summary, Ross' contribution may be divided into a positive and negative aspect. First, his observation that the reductionists were wrong in rejecting a logic of imperatives *qua* imperatives on the grounds that truth-values cannot be attributed to imperatives is correct. Certainly rules of validity operate in determining what counts as a valid inference, and not truth-values. On the other hand, however, Ross has failed to give an adequate account of imperative validity. His introducing the combination of the logic of imperative validity and the logic of satisfaction only confuses the issue. In the end it is seen that he argues that *though* imperative inference may exhibit a simple "feeling of immediacy," such inference is actually not logical. Thus there now appears a hiatus between the immediately evident nature of imperative inference, and the complex nature of such inference, which somehow lies behind the immediately evident.

Thus in breaking away from the positivists, Ross has attempted to salvage the possibility that a logic of imperatives is possible without the thorough reduction of imperatives to indicatives. What he comes out with, however, is an even more complex and difficult logic than that of his predecessors. For now one must contend with both a logic of validity and a logic of satisfaction when inferring imperatives.

H.G. Bohnert attempts to circumvent the complexity of Ross' attempt by presenting a logic of imperatives which includes the emotive quality of imperatives. He begins by decrying the up-to-now accepted intensionalist' view that because imperatives have a motivational content they cannot be inferred like indicatives. In Bohnert's view, the motivational aspect of a sentence does not "jeopardize" its truth-value, for imperatives can "play a role in derivation." By bringing out the "empirically discoverable" properties of imperatives, Bohnert believes a more formal analysis of imperatives can be presented.[88]

Thus Bohnert departs from the positivist' outlook by seeking to include within his logic the emotive quality of imperatives. On the other hand, he wants to articulate a logic which is propositional, that is a logic which deals with indicatives though augmented with the motivational aspect of commands. In this respect, Bohnert follows the reductionists. For he too reduces imperatives to indicatives, though in a way which includes their emotive element.

Bohnert proceeds by first isolating what is meant by the "motivational" element of sentences. Thus, situation M is said to motivate x, when x, upon understanding M, derives 'PvB(x)', in an exclusive sense. The latter, the "motivating disjunction," states that x behaves in manner B or x will undergo some future penalty P.[89]

The function PvB(x) is governed by the two arguments of "urgency" and of "degree of uncertainty as to appropriate reaction." Thus, as the degree of urgency increases, the mention of the mode of reaction B becomes more prominent than P. For example, someone is more likely to say to a neighbour whose house is in flames "Run," rather than "if you do not run, you are going to get burnt and you may die." Urgency, therefore, induces mention only of the kind of behaviour required, whereas uncertainty of action involves the statement of the consequence (or penalty), so as to further explicate *why* a certain reaction is required.[90]

Bohnert observes that what has thus far been taken by thinkers as the "imperative element," is actually the "unspoken penalty" a sentence may involve, and this has nothing to do with the imperator's feelings. Thus it is wrong to say, as the intensionalists have thus far maintained, that the "motivating" factor of imperatives is the reason why imperatives are meaningless. In Bohnert's view 'the imperative element' can play just as important a role in imperative derivations as the 'indicative factor.' " He goes on to present the following example :

> "Keep this car properly lubricated !
> I will not lubricate this car.
> _____
> Then this car will soon break down."

Here Bohnert says that the apparent non-logical nature of the above inference stems from the fact that the first premiss is an assumed ellipsis, which says "Either this car is properly lubricated or it will break down." Once this is brought out, the inference is seen to be logically valid. In this way Bohnert claims that the "motivating" factor plays an important part in imperative derivations.[91]

It is important to note, however, that the above inference is valid only when the ellipsis is brought out. Thus, Bohnert cannot but claim that it is the imperative as *translated into* the ellipsis which accounts for the validity of the inference. Thus also Bohnert has not clearly shown that the "motivating" factor, as it is implied by the imperative itself, plays any decisive role in imperative inference. For it is seen that he must translate the first premiss into an indicative statement about the unpleasant consequences of the first premiss, prior to his saying that the above syllogism is valid. Hence the "motivating" factor must be reshaped into some indicative form in order for it to be the statement which validates the inference. In essence, then, the "motivating" factor is just another indicative premiss which in a sense augments the premisses leading to the conclusion of the above syllogism. However, it is important to repeat that it is not the said factor as "unspoken" that accounts for the validity of this inference, but rather it is this factor in its *translation as* an ellipsis which makes the above inference valid. Bohnert speaks in vague terms so as to suggest that it makes no difference whether the ellipsis is stated or not, since he believes that the "unspoken penalty" somehow makes the inference valid. Without bringing forth the ellipsis, however, it is difficult to see how he can speak meaningfully of validly inferring imperatives.

Continuing, Bohnert says that the "content" of behavioural sentences may be defined as equivalent to declarative statements, such that the latter declarative sentences can be put in a one-to-one correspondence with commands, whose content they express. In this way, he believes he has demonstrated a functional isomorphism between commands and "certain" declarative sentences.[92]

However, here again it is not clear how Bohnert can claim that the imperative element (the implied penalty) can account for the logical derivation of imperatives, and, on the other hand, seek next to establish a relation between commands and declarative sentences expressing the motivational aspects of commands. The implication here is that imperatives must *still* be reduced to declaratives in order for them to be inferable. Yet this goes against Bohnert's general thesis that the motivational factor operates *independently* in deriving imperatives in a formal sentence.

Pursuing this thesis he says that the translation of imperatives into their isomorphic declaratives "robs commands of their unique psychological imperative character." This, he says, is to be expected, since, as the "motivating disjunction" indicates, the lesser the urgency the less truncated becomes the imperative.[93]

However, Bohnert does not take into account how an imperative can have no truncated character and still be regarded a forceful imperative. For example, a command may be expressable only in an involved way, because of the complexity of that which must be done. Yet, because the command cannot be truncated into one or two words, it does not mean that such a command is less motivating than one which may be expressed as "Run !" It seems, therefore, that there is no significant correspondence between the truncation of the means of expressing a command and the motivational (or imperatival) character of imperatives.

The case of "complex" imperatives also serves to illustrate that the "motivational disjunct" cannot be relied upon as a means of determining that which makes possible imperative inference. For where complex directives are involved, the "motivating factor" is not profoundly prominent. Thus Bohnert will either have to deny that complex imperatives are inferable, or he will have to look for something more definite to account for imperative inference.

Bohnert's aim, however, is to show that Ross is wrong in saying that a logic of imperatives involves a logic of validity and a logic of satisfaction, though fundamentally so-called imperative inferences are "pseudo-inferences." For Bohnert wants to bridge the gap between common indicative inferences and a logic of imperatives by improving upon the system of Hofstadter and McKinsey.[94]

Thus he goes on to say that, upon restricting oneself to a system "in which all commands are enforced by the same penalty, P....," then, by means of his disjunctive interpretation of commands, the system of Hofstadter and McKinsey becomes analytic. Hence, in Bohnert's view, Ic becomes identical with Carnap's Ll.[95]

'P' is then taken as a propositional constant, and the various functions of Ic are defined as follows :

Definiendum	Definiens
!S	SvP
!$\check{S}$	—SvP
+	v
=	≡
$S_1 \rightarrow !S_2$	$S_1 \supset (S_2 \text{ v } P)$
$!S_1 > !S_2$	$(S_1 \text{ v } P) . (S_1 \supset S_2)$

Bohnert observes that the primitive sentences of Ic (left) now become the primitive sentences of Ll (right). He also says that the "uneasiness one intuitively feels in seeing, ..., $!S_1 + !S_2 = !(S_1 \text{ v } S_2)$," (sic.) stems from the fact that ordinarily commands involve differing penalties, and thus each operator of the above formula seems to involve different penalties.[96]

Bohnert observes that the operator '!' is seen to be superfluous in Ic. For the imperative element is not "segregated" from Ic, but rather it is part of the calculus Ll, since P (or '!') is a constant of Ic, which means that ! is a primitive of Ll. Thus in Bohnert's view, the imperative quality as expressed by 'P', is assumed by every statement in Ic, and therefore of Ll. In this sense of every statement of Ic implying a penalty, the operator 'P' or '!' becomes superfluous.[97]

Furthermore, for Bohnert the satisfaction-functional interpretation of imperatives in Hofstadter and McKinsey's Ic is seen as untenable. Though commands may still be said to be satisfaction-functional in Ll, in the sense that an imperative is true if what it demands is satisfied, the implication between imperatives and analogous indicatives is seen to follow with a greater cogency with the introduction of P. For the indicative "the door is closed assumes that the penalty P will follow if the door is not closed, *just as* this same penalty is assumed if the command "close the door!" were not satisfied. Thus, being that the indicative and the analogous imperative assume as consequences the same penalty, they are both seen by Bohnert as implying each other in a more meaningful way, than that suggested by their being satisfaction-functional. In the author's view, however, the strangeness of this P-implication lies in that such derivation of indicatives from imperatives, and conversely, "is hardly ever used."[98]

Thus by introducing P (penalty) as a propositional constant in the system of Hofstadter and McKinsey he hopes to salvage it from the criticism that is does not express the "immediate feeling of evidence," which imperative inference 'ordinarily" appears to involve. However, Bohnert has not successfully met the indicated criticism. For Bohnert asks his reader to *assume* that 'P' is the "same penalty," which enforces all commands. Bohnert himself confessed to the artificiality of this assumption, since he grants that the above kind of logic, though augmented by P, leads to the uncommon mode of saying that the expression "the door is closed" means the imperative "close the door!" This way of speaking is the ultimate result of assuming that there is a single penalty to which all statements, whether indicatives are subject to. Apart from the implausibility of this assumption, Bohnert has not accounted for the feeling of evidence to which Ross refers. For it is not sufficient to explain this feeling in terms of penalty, since P does not explain what it means to "infer" one imperative from another.

Thus Ross' criticism still holds, since Bohnert also evades the question of *how* imperatives are formally inferred. Furthermore, though there are ambiguities in Ross' view as to how the validity of imperatives can be determined as the "possession" of a psychological state, his importance to the study of how a logic of imperatives may be evolved is undiminished. For Ross calls attention to the fact that the nature of imperative "validity" has been largely neglected by commentators. Also, in spite of its short-comings, his account of such validity reveals a deeper awareness of the problems which imperative reasoning involves, than is found with the positivists and those which follow in their tradition.

Section 2. **The Nonindicative Structure of Imperatives**

Whereas Ross ended by saying that what is ordinarily taken as an imperative inference is really a pseudo-logical inference, R.M. Hare claims that such inference is logical, though nonindicative. Both in his article "Imperative Sentences." and his book *The Language of Morals*, Hare argues that imperatives can be inferred from other imperatives *without* any reference to so-called "corresponding" sentences[99]. In "Imperative Sentences", Hare admonishes the reductionists for confining themselves only to indicative sentences when attempting to evolve logics of imperatives. In his view the "logical behaviour" of imperatives is the same as that of indicatives.[100] Thus Hare is seen to depart from the positivists insofar as he seeks the logic of imperatives as completely parallel to the logic of indicatives.

Fundamentally, Hare takes imperatives as dealing with "states of affairs," which are brought about through action ("praxis") and doing ("poiesis"). A question about a command thus involves one's deliberating about some alternative course of action. This again illustrates how imperatives are to be distinguished from indicatives. For a question about an indicative deals with whether there are factual alternatives relevant to some particular situation. This is certainly not the case with questions dealing with imperatives, wherein no factual claim is made.[101]

In contrast to these differences, Hare proceeds to show how an imperative and an indicative are alike. Thus he considers the imperative "(1) Mary, please show Mrs. Prendergast her room." and the indicative "(2) Mary will show you your room, Mrs. Prendergast." Both (1) and (2) refer to the "description" of the same complex series of events, which is the showing of the room to Mrs. Prendergast by Mary. This description itself is *not* a sentence, since the event described is not said to have happened or that it would happen, or even that because it is commanded it occurs.[102]

Reflecting on the criterion which Hare uses to turn the above description into a sentence, it seems odd for him to insist that the completion of the described imperative, or even the intimation as to when it will be completed, suffices to turn this description into a sentence. Essentially, the idea of "sentence" is a syntactical notion, relating a subject to an object by means of a verb. Though semantics may play a role in defining "sentence," insofar as some meaning must be given to "subject," "object", and "predicate," the defining criteria of "sentence" itself is not the realisation of

an action. Hare states, however, that the expression "Showing of the room to Mrs. Prendergast by Mary at time t" is
not a sentence because no action is relevant to it, but it is
characterized as "words." However, this expression cannot
"just" be words, since there is a definite action indicated
here occurring at a definite time t. If this phrase were only
words, then one could say nothing about it not even that it is
a phrase. Nonetheless, one can say something about its meaning, and in fact it is found by Hare to be that about which
imperative (1) and indicative (2) are about. Actually, this expression is a laconic means of referring to the kind of action
which imperative (1) and indicative (2) involve. Thus a
proper rendition of it will include the fact that (1) and (2)
concern themselves with "the showing of the room to Mrs.
Prendergast by Mary." In this way one still ends up with
a sentence, which explains what (1) and (2) deal with. As
it stands in Hare's account, the 'descriptions' of what (1)
and (2) are said to be about cannot describe anything, since
there is no subject or predicate to which it is applicable.

What is most disturbing about Hare's thesis is that he
says "Showing of the room to Mrs. Prendergast by Mary at
time t" is a "description." For as S.E. Toulmin and
K. Baier point out in their article "On Describing," a 'description' in an ordinary sense involves a variety of things,
among which are considerations about what it is that is
being described, the position of the speaker to the persons
hearing his description, the function or purpose of the description, etc. These writers correctly point out that giving
a description is a "complex affair." All questions which
arise with respect to descriptions deal with the adequacy of
the description, that is, is it accurate, one-sided, misleading,
correct in its information, etc. Such questions about descriptions, according to Toulmin and Baier, measure the
"success" of the description.[103] In view of this, it is not
unreasonable to question the plausibility of a "description"
such as the one proposed by Hare, wherein there is no
employment of the sentential means of expression. One
may seriously doubt the "success" which Hare's kind of

description achieves, in view of the exclusion of employing sentences to express what is described.

It is important to dwell on the point of the grammatical nature of the expression : "Showing of the room to Mrs. Prendergast by Mary." For it is evident that Hare is trying hard to avoid saying that both (1) and (2) are reducible to a *sentence* about the showing of the room to Mrs. Prendergast by Mary. If he were to say that this expression was a sentence then he would be doing exactly the same thing he accuses the positivists of doing, that is, reducing imperatives to indicative sentences. Thus Hare tries to stay clear of saying that imperative (1) is reducible to a sentence. Yet he pays a heavy price for doing this, since he ends up by saying that (1) is *about* a description, about which the only thing that can be said syntactically is that it is made up of "words." Yet can this then be an acceptable *description ?*

Hare goes on to consider how a logic of imperatives may be evolved in view of what he has said thus far. For this purpose he introduces some new terms, which he further clarifies in *The Language of Morals*. However, as will be seen, because nothing new is gained by these refinements, the terminology used in his article will be preserved in expounding his position.

Hare says that both (1) and (2) above describe the series of events designated by "showing of the room to Mrs. Prendergast by Mary." This Hare calls the "descriptive function" of (1) and (2). That "part of" a sentence which does the describing he terms the "descriptor" of an indicative or an imperative. Hence if one includes the descriptor of (1) one would have : "(1.1) Showing of her room to Mrs. Prendergast by Mary at time t, *yes.*" The descriptor of (1.1) would be 'Showing of her room to Mrs. Prendergast by Mary at time t.' This is the same descriptor as that of say (2.1).[104]

Sentences (1.1) and (2.1) differ with respect to their "dictors," that is, with respect to "please" and "yes." For

these latter two words "really do the *saying* ... which a
sentence does." In (1.1) the imperative dictor *commands*
what is described by the imperative descriptor. However,
in (2.1) the indicative dictor (yes) says that what is described
by the descriptor *is the case*.[105] In short it can be said that
the dictor of a sentence indicates the linguistic function
of the sentence with respect to what its descriptor describes.

In *The Language of Morals*, Hare attempts to clarify
what he means by a descriptor and a dictor. He calls the
descriptor of a sentence the "phrastic" part of the sentence.
This he takes from the Greek *phrazo*, meaning "to point
out." He then calls the dictor of a sentence the "neustic"
part of a sentence. This again he takes from the Greek
nefstazo, meaning to agree or "nod assent." However,
nothing much is gained by alluding to the Greek forms of a
descriptor and a dictor.[106] The introduction of the Greek
indicates somewhat clearer that the descriptor is a kind of
phrase. However, this is also suggested in the explanation
given by Hare in "Imperative Sentences." Thus, the terminology of the earlier essay can be retained.

Having indicated that imperatives and indicatives may
be alike with respect to their descriptors, Hare proceeds to
develop the logic of imperatives on the basis of the
descriptum of imperatives and indicatives. For this purpose he presents two syllogisms, one containing solely
indicatives and the other only imperatives, but both being
the same insofar as they have the same descriptors operating. Thus the syllogism :

> A.   You will use an axe or a saw.
>   You will not use an axe.
> _____
>   You will use a saw.

ma   be translated with the proper descriptor and dictor as:

> B.   Use of axe or saw by you shortly, yes.
>   No use of axe by you shortly, yes.
> _____
>   Use of saw by you shortly, yes.

or A may be translated into its proper descriptor and dictor
as :

> C.   Use of axe or saw by you shortly, please.
>
> No use of axe by you shortly, please.
>
> ───────────────────────────────────
>
> Use of saw by you shortly, please.

Hence in that B and C differ only with respect to their
dictors: "yes" and "please" respectively, and since the dictors do not play a role in the arguments of the syllogisms,
both B and C may be written as :

> D.   Use of axe or saw by you shortly.
>
> No use of axe by you shortly.
>
> ───────────────────────────────────
>
> Use of saw by you shortly.

Thus D is really what makes syllogism B and C the same,
and one can add any of the dictors of B and C to D so as
to come out with B or C.[107]

What Hare has actually done is to isolate and then by-
pass the emotive quality (the sense of urgency) of imperatives. For one of the enormous problems involved in
developing a logic of imperatives is to account for the
imperative element within such a logic. Here, however,
Hare says that the imperative dictor, which is little else
than the element of urgency and demand imperatives
ordinarily manifest, is unimportant for the argument of
syllogism C. Thus he thinks he can develop a logic of
imperatives from the point of view of a general logic of
descriptive propositions. However, one can charge Hare
with the same error Ross attributes to Jörgensen, where
Ross says that the latter (Jörgensen) evades the problem of
how imperatives may be inferred by assuming that imperatives can be reduced to indicatives, and thus the logic of
indicatives is the logic of imperatives. In the same way,
Hare does not face the question of *how* an imperative may
be inferred from another imperative. Rather, Hare goes
around this issue by alluding to problematic "descriptions"
which somehow express the content of both imperatives and

indicatives, and which as "indicatives" account for imperative inference.

A further objection to Hare's view of how imperative reasoning takes place is found in Robert G. Turnbull's Article "A Note on Mr. Hare's 'Logic of Imperatives.' " Turnbull considers how Hare can maintain that imperatives, like indicatives, are descriptorily (or phrastically) valid, while in *The Language of Morals* he sets down the following two rules, which govern *sentential* validity :

"(1)   No indicative conclusion can be validly drawn from a set of premisses which cannot be validly drawn from the indicatives among them alone.

(2)   No imperative conclusion can be validly drawn from a set of premisses which does not contain at least one imperative."

For Turnbull observes that Hare holds that *most* inferences, meaning *all* inferences, are descriptorly valid, and yet mentions the above two rules in connection with the valid inferring of imperative *sentences* or indicative *sentences*. Thus there seems to be a "bifurcation" of validity in Hare's position generally. For, on the one hand, Hare speaks of sentential validity, including both indicative and imperative sentences, and on the other hand, he speaks of descriptoral validity, referring to the inference of a descriptor from other descriptors. Turnbull also observes that an inference may be descriptorily valid and yet be sententially invalid. For it would make no difference in Hare's view if, with regard to descriptoral validity, an argument has indicative premisses and an imperative conclusion. However, such an argument is invalid with respect to sentential validity. Thus these two kinds of validity are a source of incongruity from an overall view of Hare's position.[108]

In "Imperative Sentences" Hare goes on to give a "formal" statement covering the mode of reasoning found in imperative and indicative reasoning. Thus he says that if 'C' stands for a command, and 'S' stands for a statement having the same descriptor as 'C,' then where c_1, c_2...c_n are commands inferable from 'C' (meaning that c_1, c_2,.. are true if the states of affairs designated by descriptor of 'C' is the case), then to command C is to command c_1, c_2,...c_n . Analogously a_1, a_2,...a_n may be said to be inferred from B. However, one cannot infer S from s_1, nor can he infer C from c_1, though the converse is true.[109]

In spite of Hare's attempt to strengthen his view, it falls prey to the incisive criticism of R.F. Peters. For the latter first questions the plausibility of Hare's saying that imperatives may "contradict" each other. Though it may be possible to speak in terms of one command countermanding another, it is incorrect English usage to speak of commands contradicting each other. The latter idea is properly applicable only to indicatives. Furthermore, the notion of "contradiction," as employed by Hare, is even more problematic where one considers the fact that he (Hare) does not regard imperatives as true or false. It is recalled that Hare does not regard the description denoted by the imperative as a sentence. Hence as non-sentences imperatives in Hare's view cannot be true or false. Here Peters notes that if imperatives cannot be said to be true or false, then it is difficult to see how imperatives can be said to contradict.[110]

Extending Peter's criticism to one of Hare's so-called 'syllogisms,' it is seen that there is now a question as to what Hare is able to infer. For if commands are taken as countermanding each other in some contexts, then the command "Use an axe or a saw" is countermanded by the command "Do not use an axe !" Thus Hare cannot infer from these two premises (so-called) the conclusion (so-called) "Use a saw !" Though he may object that the second command only countermands one disjunct of the first command, yet it is still true that the first command is an exclusive disjunction, and as such it is in some sense denied by the second premiss. This becomes evident from the fact that it is not unjustified for the agent in this case to *ask* whether the imperator wants him to use a saw. At least it must be granted by Hare that the status of the first command has become confused with the introduction of the second command, to the point where one can say that the first command is now countermanded. Thus it is difficult to see what sort of inference can result from these two commands.

Peters also attacks Hare's contention that the nature of imperative inference transcends the mood in which premisses are in. It is recalled that one of Hare's basic points is that imperative and indicative inference deals with the content of the descriptor, and not with the dictor. Thus it is possible to turn an indicative argument into an imperative argument by adding an imperative dictor to the description of the indicative premisses and conclusion. This he attempts to illustrate by using the imperative dictor "let" in the following case :

> "Let all men be mortal.
> Let Socrates be a man.
> _____
> Let Socrates be mortal."

Peters objects to the above on the grounds that it by no means becomes apparent how by one's commanding that all men be mortal, and that Socrates be a man, then the imperator is reasoning or proving that Socrates be mortal. For it seems more natural to say that the imperator is commanding the conclusion. However, to command a conclusion is to do something different than to reason a conclusion. In the latter case one can always "justify" his reasoning by alluding to accepted rules of inference or validity. In the case of one's commanding a conclusion there need be no other justification than that the imperator commands the conclusion. Thus it does appear to make a difference in one's mode of arguing when the imperative dictor is substituted for the indicative dictor.[111]

Duncan-Jones, in "Assertions and Commands," attempts to salvage aspects of Hare's position. Essentially, he seeks to preserve Hare's view that imperative inference reflects indicative reasoning. For he holds that imperatives "implicitly" contain indicatives. However, Duncan-Jones departs from Hare in the way he attempts to show how imperatives. contain indicatives. For it is in the way that commands reflect a "justification" which allows for one to extract the indicative aspects of commands. Duncan-Jones employs the following example to illustrate his point :

> "In the event of matches being near you,
> handing them by you to me, Please.
> Matches being near you, Yes.
>
> ―――――――――――――――――――――――
>
> Handing of matches by you to me, Please"

He holds that the second premiss of the above syllogism is *implicit* in the first, which is an imperative. However, this "implicitness" is revealed by the fact that both premisses are analogous because they involve a similar "responsive attitude" on the part of the imperator of premiss one, and agent to premiss two.[112] However, he does not go very far in explaining just what exactly is meant by "responsive attitude," and why the latter should form the basis for an analogy between commands and indicatives. Nonetheless, for Duncan-Jones this responsive attitude takes the place of the descriptor in Hare's position, and it allows for the justification of both of the above premisses. For in the above example, the first premiss includes that the agent consents to hand over the matches if they are nearby. Thus the second premiss is implicit in the first, since the first premiss is said to imply that the matches are near the said person, and this person has the same responsive attitude towards the second premiss as he has towards the first.[113]

In spite of the claimed obviousness of the implicitness of premiss two in premiss one, it is not clear how from the stated "condition" of the first premiss, that is, "In the event of..." Duncan-Jones can arrive at the indicative that something is the case, that is, "Matches being near you, yes." No amount of conjuring can explain how there is the same "responsive attitude" with respect to both premisses. In fact, it does not seem sensible to claim that an imperative can elicit the same attitude as an indicative, and conversely. Finally, the conclusion of the syllogism does not clearly stand out as an imperative. For it cannot be an imperative, since, as Duncan-Jones explicitly states, it "is to be understood as the sort of command which might be given without any reference to the limitations of the actual world, ..."[114] Hence the question arises, what kind of imperative has Duncan-Jones in mind which "might be given," and which is not affected by the "limitations of the actual world ?" Here one can object to his view, just as Peters objects to Hare's position on imperative inference. For like Hare, Duncan-Jones has not shown that the conclusion of the syllogism he presents is an imperative, as it ought to be if his account of imperative reasoning is correct.

In retrospect, Hare's attempt at presenting a logic of imperatives fails because he is not able to arrive at a suitable mid-ground to which he can reduce both imperatives and indicatives, without holding all imperatives uniformally reducible to indicatives. This is seen in his inability to give an adequate characterization of the nature of the description which he claims both imperatives and indicatives reflect. Thus also, Hare's avoidance of the view that imperatives are reducible to indicatives renders his account of imperative inference highly problematic.

Yet in the perspective being considered, Hare's contributions represent an important facet of the movement away from the treatment of the issue by positivists. For Hare looks closer at the imperative itself, and sees a complex compound of a descriptor complemented by a dictor, with the former taken as designating a description common to imperatives and indicatives alike, and the latter being the means whereby one distinguishes imperatives from indicatives. Thus the imperative, as a grammatical entity, is more involved than the positivists supposed it to be.

It may be argued that because Hare speaks in terms of the descriptor "designating" a description, his analysis of imperatives is thus extensional rather than intensional. Though Hare does refer to the *denotatum* of the descriptor, he is also seen to distinguish imperatives from indicatives on the basis of their respected dictors. The latter, expressed by the words "please" and "yes", indicate the context in which a certain description is expressed. Thus Hare's means of defining imperatives relies on the *context* in which they occur. For this reason therefore, Hare is properly included among those who derive the meaning of imperatives from their respective intensional analysis.

Generally, Hare's work differs from that of Ross. Hare concentrates upon the structure of imperatives *qua* imperatives, rather than upon how imperative inference relates to indicative inference. In Hare's view both these kinds of inference are the same. In spite of this difference both recognize the deficiencies in the view of the reductionists. In short, both realize that imperatives are much too complex to be simply reduced to indicatives.

Section 3. Validity and Imperative Reasoning

The question of how imperatives may be said to form *valid* arguments is first raised by Alf Ross. However, in *The Open Society and Its Enemies*, Karl Popper also attempts to account for imperative validity, and fares no better than Ross. However, Popper departs from Ross in that he bases his notion of validity on the "fact" of one's satisfying or not satisfying a norm or imperative. Ross is seen to base imperative validity on the psychological state imperatives connote.

Popper points out that, though imperatives are not derivable from factual statements, imperatives do have an informative meaning, which is other than that of being descriptive of some psychological state. He holds that an imperative is valid because it can be traced back to a statement which says that the imperative has been obeyed. Only in this way can imperatives be said to be derived from facts. Thus their derivatives from facts is tantamount to deriving the statement : "Napoleon died on St. Helena," from the fact that a statement saying that Napoleon did die on St. Helena is true.[116]

Thus Popper believes he can argue for the validity of the

imperative "Don't steal !" by inferring it from "Mr. A forbids stealing, and Mr. A's prohibition is valid (obeyed)." According to Popper, the validity of imperatives arises from a relational property, which is analogous to that of truth or falsity in judgments. This is the property of obedience or nonobedience of commands. Popper bases this analogy on the apparent similarity in the way in which one has to search for *external* proof so as to ascertain the truth of judgments. For one must also look outside a command to see whether or not it has been obeyed.[117]

Commenting upon Popper's position, A.N. Prior states in *Logic and the Basis of Ethics*, that in analytic propositions like " 'Something human is non-human.' " one need not go "outside" the proposition in order to determine whether it is true or not. Thus also, one knows the command : " 'Do what you will not do!' " will be disobeyed without having to go out of the command so as to verify it. Thus Popper's analogy between truth and falsehood, and obedience and nonobedience, does not stand the test. Furthermore, the analogy leads to saying that " 'Mr. A's prohibition is valid.' " means (in an extensional sense), that "What Mr. A. forbids (stealing) does not occur." However, this latter sentence only enables one to infer, "Stealing does not occur," which is not a command.[118]

The rejection of Popper's notion of validity by Prior reflects a pre-supposition common to all the intensionalists discussed thus far within this chapter. This is the assumption that an imperative must, in some way, relate to some outside state of affairs or events, which makes the imperative either meaningful or valid. This assumption underlies Popper's thesis where he says that the obedience or nonobedience of a command determines the command's validity. Similarly, Hare's central view that the descriptor of an imperative describes an event reflects this assumed relation of an imperative to an event. Bohnert's position also posits an outside state of affairs, namely a punishment or some penalty, which gives both meaning and importance to the emotive quality of imperatives. Finally, Ross holds that the possession of a psychological state accounts for the validity of imperatives.

Thus, these philosophers, in rejecting the positivists reduction of imperatives to indicatives, have emerged with the still greater difficulty of relating states of affairs or events to imperatives. In this respect, P. F. Strawson's views offer a general criticism of this movement away from positivism. Strawson's position in the article "Truth," arising from a general criticism of Austin's notion of "truth," states that philosophers often confuse *the question* about what a notion like "command" means with *the meaning* of this notion itself. For they posit *undefined* entities, such as events or state of affairs, to "explain" what is meant by a command. However, the questions which arise after these "explanations" are given deal with just how these entities can be spoken of as relating to the imperatives they are said to explain. In short, those who attempt to depart from the positivist' reduction of imperatives end up with words like "events" or "states of affairs," which contain the problem of how imperatives should be defined. Such thinkers fail to take notice that in using these words, one is using terms which have a kind of 'word-world-relating discourse...*built in* to them."[119] Thus to refer only to "states-of-affairs" or "events" in the manner of Ross and Hare, for example, does not explain how imperatives relate to them in ordinary discourse.

Furthermore, as the criticism of these authors has shown, it is with respect to the nature of the entities they posit : mental states, fear of punishment, events, etc. that doubts about their views are raised. For, in positing what they do, these thinkers fail to explain how they have accounted for imperatives. The only thing they have succeeded in showing is that imperatives, because they somehow involve these entities, are more complex in meaning than the positivists supposed.

4

Recent Intensional Logics of Imperatives : Castaneda, Von Wright, Rescher and Simon

Hector-Neri Castaneda best introduces the discussions which follow by observing that major contributions thus far have erroneously assumed that a logic of imperatives should be modeled upon a logic of indicative propositions : *"...una presuposicion falsa : la do que los imperativos tienen una logicidad paralela a la de los indicativos."*[120]   In Castaneda's view, as well as in the views of Von Wright, N. Rescher, and Herbert Simon : the logical structure of imperative reasoning can best be captured by employing the powerful techniques of logic, rather than to reduce imperatives into indicatives, as has been the case. In this way these later writers hope to preserve the illusive emotive character of imperatives, within a genuine calculus of imperatives.

However, without immediately entering into the way in which these men attack the problem of developing a logic of imperatives, it is important to view their contributions in light of what has already been said.   Thus, on the whole, the writers discussed below are aware of the insufficiencies of the past imperative logics, especially with respect to their failure at expressing the subtleties which imperatives are found to possess.   For this reason these thinkers emphasize the power of logic, as an analytical tool, to express what imperative reasoning involves.   Evident with these writers, therefore, is a confidence in the applicability of formal logic to imperatival analysis. Though their approach is reminiscent of Menger's, insofar as the latter sought to employ a sufficiently powerful logic to accommodate aspects of imperative reasoning, the advances in logic which are available to the former were not at Menger's disposal. Also, whereas the intensionalists thus far discussed look into the connotative meaning of imperatives, those discussed below emphasize the sense in which imperatives can be "translated" into a formal language. However, insofar as the latter also present contextualist analyses, they too fall within the general approach of evolving a logic of imperatives intensionally.

Hence within the above perspective, the views of Castaneda, Von Wright, Rescher and Simon will be presented. Also, insofar as these thinkers consider some aspects of one another's work, some relations between their approaches will be brought forth. Essentially, however, the works of each of these men reflect differences in technique, and thus it is best to treat them individually, rather than in total relation to each other.

Section 1.   Castaneda's Normative Logic N_1*

Castaneda's work in developing a logic of imperatives arises from his interest in ethics, and in particular in the notion of 'ought.' Because his work is heavily involved in criticism of this idea, and especially with his criticism of Hare's view on this notion, care must be given to seek out that which pertains to his logic of imperatives, as emerging from his views on the moral sense of 'ought.'

Castaneda's views on imperatives are presented in four major articles : "A Note on Imperative Logic," "Imperative Reasonings," *"Un Sistema General de Logica Normativa,"* and in "Imperatives, Decisions, and Oughts." These works illustrate a development in Castaneda's thought, which is that of departing from Hare's conception of a logic of imperatives, and, in his third article, presenting a logic of imperatives as being "part of" a larger logic of norms, and finally in the fourth article above, clarifying the central notions of 'norm,' 'imperative,' 'imperative inference', etc.[121]

Beginning with the first of these articles, Castaneda sets out to show the exact way his approach towards developing a logic of imperatives differs from that of Hare's. He observes that Hare argues for the logicality of imperatives by adopting the proposition : "There is a logic of sentences of type t if and only if sentences of type t can be used as premisses or conclusions of (valid) inferences." Certainly, the type t sentence Hare alludes to here would be the descriptoral phrase of imperative sentences. Furthermore, implicit in Hare's view, according to Castaneda, is the rejection of the proposition that "...imperatives are neither premisses nor conclusions of (valid) inferences," and that "A premise as well as a conclusion of a (valid) inference is either true or false." The rejection of these last propositions are in keeping with Hare's general view that it no longer makes a difference whether imperatives or indicatives form parts of a syllogism, since the (value-neutral) descriptive phrases of both indicatives and imperatives alone play a role in any sort of inference.[122]

Castaneda characterizes his own view as in one sense simpler, and in another sense more complex than Hare's. In the first place Castaneda holds the following argument

"...1. There is a logic of sentences of type t if and only if sentences of type t can be used as premisses or conclusions of (valid) inferences.

2. A premiss as well as a conclusion of a (valid) inference is either true or false.

3. Imperatives are neither true nor false.

4. Therefore, imperatives are neither premisses nor conclusions of (valid) inferences.

5. In consequence, there is no logic of imperatives..."[123]

However, though he holds the above argument he also wants to maintain that there is a kind of "semi-logic" of

imperatives.   The latter logic is constructed on a meta-logic
of imperatives, that is, "...a systematization of the rules
allowing the inference of meta-indicatives asserting that a
certain imperative is justified or obeyed or fulfilled from a
set of other indicatives."   Castaneda's own logic of imperatives, however, differs from the above meta-logic in that it
is a "semi-logic" of imperatives, which is "part of the formation rules for normatives in a system containing indicatives."[124]

Thus Castaneda sees the logic of imperatives as somehow included within a larger logic of norms, and not, contrary to Hare, as being "part of" a general logic of indicatives.   In Castaneda's view, the norm "X ought to do A"
is an indicative which constitutes a modal sentence "formed
out of the imperative" 'X, do A !' by means of the modal
operator "ought," which is akin to Lewis' operator '$\square$' or
'must.'[125]

In this way, Castaneda can hold the second and the
fourth propositions of the above argument, and still maintain that there is an imperative logic, albeit fragmentary
and dependent upon a normative logic.   Here Castaneda
adds that a logic along the lines proposed by him illustrates
the exact "kinship between imperatives and normatives."
Throughout Castaneda considers this "kinship" obvious,
since he observes that the 'reasons' for an ethical judgment
(or norm) "support the judgment in the way that reasons
support imperatives."[126]

The simplicity of Castaneda's logic of imperatives, as
opposed to that of Hare's, lies in the fact that it involves
no problem as to how to reconcile the requirement that a
premiss and a conclusion of a valid inference must be either
true or false, and the fact that imperatives can be neither
premisses nor conclusions of valid inferences.   Castaneda
believes he has gotten around this problem by admittingly
complicating the very idea of a logic of imperatives, in that
he takes it as dependent upon a logic of norms. For imperatives form norms, which are essentially modal indicatives,
by means of the modal operator "ought."   Thus by con-

centrating upon the general logic of norms, which is by Castaneda's own definition a logic of indicatives, one would thereby capture the logic of imperatives, the latter being, again by definition, "part of the formation rules for normatives in a system containing indicatives."

Though strong criticism of Castaneda's logic of imperatives at this point would be premature, nonetheless something can be said about his procedure, and whether in fact he has escaped the difficulties which beset Hare's contentions. First it may be asked how a logic of norms be formulated, if that from which norms are formed, namely imperatives, remain undefined as to the way they function in a formal system. In proceeding as he does Castaneda is assuming that the logic of imperatives will shine through the logic of norms. Yet what is the basis for this assumption ? Castaneda says that in ethics there is a kinship in the way reasons support norms and how reasons support imperatives. And because of this kinship his procedure assumes that the formulating of a logic of norms, preempts, so to speak, a logic of imperatives. However, Castaneda does not explain how a logic of imperatives of this kind applies in other non-ethical fields of intercourse. Indeed, the question arises as to the "usefulness" of Castaneda's logic of imperatives apart from ethics.

Also, if the elemental aspects of norms are imperatives, as Castaneda claims, then is it not a "better" procedure to concentrate first upon the logic of imperatives, and from this to go on and develop a logic of norms ? To present a logic of imperatives in Castaneda's manner overcomplicates the primary objective of arriving at only a logic of imperatives, and creates the added and unnecessary problem of explaining why a logic of imperatives must be in some way presupposed by a logic of norms.

However, careful attention must be given to the exposition of his system, as he expounds it in 'Un Sistema General de Logica Normatiya," "Imperative Reasonings," and "Imperatives, Decisions, and "Oughts"." After which additional criticism of Castaneda's position can be given.

In the first of the three articles Castaneda states that in his logic of imperatives the issues which plague previous logics do not arise. To illustrate this greater simplicity of his logic he on the one hand investigates the relation which exists between norms and imperatives, and on the other hand looks into the relations between norms and descriptive propositions or indicatives. In essence, the investigation which follows deals with the nature of the relation between is and ought ("...*entre el ser y el deber ser*..."). It is towards the precise clarification of this relation that his investigations are directed. Thus also, to view the entire problem of formulating a logic of imperatives in terms of "is" and "ought" according to Castaneda, is to presuppose the assimilation of the logic of imperatives by the logic of norms. Exactly how such an assimilation comes about is explained in the articulation of his logic.[127]

Castaneda sees the general objective of his logic as also the *systematic* clarification of the *logical* relation between norms, imperatives, and descriptive indicative propositions. This clarification results from exhibiting the formal structure of norms in general, without regard to particular norms, such as those found in legal contexts, sociology, etc.[128]

Prior to embarking upon the presentation of a logic of norms, he elects to give an informal analysis of the characteristics of ordinary norms, which he admittedly imprecisely *intuits* norms as possessing. The following characteristics, therefore, are what he thinks are common to all norms :

"1. Norms, imperatives and ordinary descriptive propositions are three forms of speech, which are not reducible to each other.

2. Imperative utterances are neither true nor false, nor can imperatives serve as premisses or conclusions in any reasoning.

3. Norms, on the other hand, may serve as premisses or conclusions in reasoning. For example :

> If Charles is studying, then you must leave him alone.
>
> Charles is studying.
>
> ———————————————————————————
>
> Therefore : You must leave him (Charles) alone !

4. On the one hand there are norms which are applicable or must be obeyed, and on the other hand there are others that cannot be obeyed.

5. To every normative utterance there corresponds an ordinary indicative utterance. For example :

   > "All must say the truth."———"All say the truth."

6. Norms and their corresponding ordinary indicative utterances are mutually uninferrable, that is to say, it is invalid by any means of reasoning to have either norms or their indicatives as their premises, and their counterparts as conclusions.

7. To every norm there corresponds an imperative :

   > "John must sleep."———"John, sleep !"

8. In some sense, norms include or assimilate imperatives.

9. In part, this assimilation (between norms and imperatives) consists in that : (1) neither imperatives nor norms have the universe for their object of discourse, and (2) both types of propositions have for their object the influencing of the conduct of individuals.

10. This last characteristic (9), in the case of norms, is akin to the *acceptance* that "I must do A." (that is, the sincere belief that I have to do A) induces me to A.

11. Some kinds of norms indicate that the corresponding imperative is reasonable or justifiable."[129]

For Castaneda the above are the most notable characteristics norms are found to reflect in ordinary discourse.
However, he notes that he is interested only in the first
eight of these characteristics, since they are the most clearly
formal ("*formales*") properties of norms. Characteristics
(9) and (10) are not considered by him to be formal, however, their explanation will not be entered into. Finally,
the last characteristic is formal, though its complexity also
warrants a future discussion in Castaneda's view.[130]

Before passing on to Castaneda's presentation of system
N_1*, it is helpful to examine the plausibility of the above
characteristics he "intuits" norms to possess.

The first interesting point which can be raised is how,
if by characteristic (1), norms, imperatives, and descriptive
propositions are irreducible to each other, can a norm, by
characteristic (3), be part of a chain of reasoning, either as
a premiss or a conclusion. For it appears that if a norm is
to function either as a conclusion or as a premiss of an
inference, then such a norm must be in some sense true or
false. (It has already been shown in considering Castaneda's
first article that he accepts truth and falsehood to be
characteristics of premisses or conclusions of inference.)
However, if norms are now taken as true or false, how
different are they from descriptive propositions, to which,
by (1), they (norms) cannot be reduced ? For example, in
characteristic (3) Castaneda uses the conditional : "If
Charles is studying, then you must leave him alone," as a
norm in an inference. Yet it may be said that such a norm
is a conditional description of a state of affairs, which is a
true description if in fact Charles is studying. Thus that
this "norm" in (3) is true or false depends upon considering
it as a descriptive proposition, which *facts* substantiate or
falsify. In itself, a norm, having the model operator
"must," is not ostensively verifiable. It is only when the
norm is taken as a description of some sought that it can
be said to be true or false. Yet to so reduce norms to
descriptive propositions violates Castaneda's first *intuited*
characteristic of norms.

Related to the above point against Castaneda's conception of norms is an objection to his fifth characteristic of norms. For he claims that there "corresponds ("*corresponde*") an ordinary indicative utterance to every norm." Thus given the example of the norm "All must say the truth" there corresponds to this the indicative "All say the truth."[131] Yet one might ask what is the nature of this "correspondence," and what is the real nature of this "indicative utterance ?" Castaneda does not explain the sense in which "correspondence" is to be taken. For this cannot be a correspondence in the sense that the truth of the norm determines the truth of the corresponding indicative and conversely, since in that case norms may be again reducible to indicatives, in violation of characteristic (1). Furthermore, it is quite possible to act upon the norm that "All must say the truth," though the evidence is overwhelming to the effect that the statement "All say the truth" is false. Here again, there is a problem as to how the above norm is said by Castaneda to correspond to its indicative. Perhaps he takes "corresponds" here in the sense that "the action" suggested by the norm is suggested as well by the indicative to which the norm corresponds. However, this possibility is also unacceptable since the action of telling the truth expressed in the norm is not the same action of telling the truth in the so-called corresponding indicative sentence. For in the case of the norm, the expressed action of telling the truth is essentially an individual and future-time action, since the norm in a sense commands each individual it is directed to say the truth. On the other hand, the action conveyed by the corresponding indicative is really a nonactualized and nonactualizable action. Thus there are differences between these two actions, conveyed by the respected norm and indicative utterance.

In proceeding on to his system N_1*, Castaneda states that he is primarily concerned with showing the structure of norms, and in particular the way in which norms include imperatives. As a step in this direction he again considers the way in which it can be said of a norm that it is true or false, in a way similar to how an indicative is said to be true or false. For he sees nothing "abnormal" in saying that norms are justified or unjustified, though certain "complications" arise when one compares the justification of norms with the truth values of indicatives. Thus he says in order to speak of norms as having truth values, like descriptive propositions, norms must be considered much like "indicative utterances."[132]

Castaneda is keenly aware of the difficulties involved in attributing truth values to imperatives. For in "Imperative Reasonings" he specifically makes reference to the difficulties encountered by others in attempting to attach the same kind of truth values to imperatives, as one attaches to indicatives. For this reason he proposes that the proper way of explaining imperatival implication is by looking at the broader picture in which imperatives are set, and to attempt to indicate th conditions and circumstances under which it would be *appropriate* for one to obey an imperative.[133] In this way he seeks to re-emphasize his earlier view that it is only by means of a logic of normatives (or ought statements) that one attains a logic of imperatives.

In Castaneda's view, also, the basic difference between imperatives and descriptive propositions (including norms) is in the mode (*modo*) they each combine their subject and predicate. Furthermore, as characteristics 5. and 7. above state, this difference in mode can be ultimately reduced to the same indicative proposition. Hence he proceeds to characterize the difference between the mode of combining the subject and predicate in imperatives and how they are combined in descriptive indicatives. For illustration, in the case of the descriptive proposition : "Louis looks for John," the mode of combining subject to predicate shall be presented by means of parentheses, thus it will illustrate by the following expression : "To look for (Louis, John)." On the other hand, the mode whereby the combination of subject and predicate take place in imperatives shall be illustrated by means of brackets. Thus in the case of "Louis, look for John !" the conjunction of subject and predicate is expressed as "To look for [Louis, John]."[134]

The above distinction in the use of parentheses and brackets is of importance in that it will help illustrate that norms contain imperatives. For Castaneda holds that there is an intimate relation between norms and imperatives, though this is a *constitutive* relation, and *not* an inferential relation. The way in which it is a constitutive relation evolves around the explanation of the function of the word 'ought' (*debemos*).[135]

Castaneda observes that when one applies the word 'ought' as a logical term with its inflections to an indicative proposition another new proposition results. Thus, for example,

" "Charles gives the book to John."———Give
                              (Charles, book, John).

"Charles, give the book to John."———Give
                              [Charles, book, John].

"Charles, ought to give the book to John."
                    (Give [Charles, book, John])."

He maintains that the way in which the introduction of "ought to" in the last case turns the imperative (second case) into a norm is a fact of discourse which transgresses all languages. Thus it is towards the clarification of this general feature of norms that his system N_1^* is directed.[136]

The indefinable individual primitive expressions of N_1^* are thus :

(a) Proper names or individual constants : 'a', 'b', 'c',...

(b) Individual variables : 'x', 'y', 'z', 'x_1', 'y_1', 'x_2',...

(c) Terms denotative of properties (that is, qualities and relations) : 'A', 'B',...

(d) General logical expressions : '—' (which denote negation), 'v' (which denotes alteration or disjunction *(que expresa disjunction mixta;* imperativo-*indicativa)*.

(e) Imperative logical operators : 'I' (which serves for referring us to corresponding ordinary indicatives of imperatives or norms), 'K' (which is equivalent to the use of the word 'ought' as explained above).

(f) Other signs : ' (' , ') ' , ' [' , '] '.

Castaneda proceeds to give some formal rules for the formation of meaningful utterances in N_1^*.[137]

*(2) Rule for the formation of utterances :

(A) The expressions of the following forms *are indicatives*, and are the only indicatives of N_1^* :

(a) $Z(Y)$, where Z is a qualitative predicate and Y a proper name or an individual variable; $Z^n (Y_1 Y_2,...,Y^n)$, where Z^n is a relative predicate of n terms and Y_1, Y_2,...,Y^n are constants or individual variables.

(b) $-(Z)$, where Z is an indicative.

(c) $(X) (Z)$, where Z is on indicative and X is an individual variable.

(d) (Z) v (Y), where Z and Y are indicatives.

(e) $I (Z)$, where Z is an imperative.

(f) $K (Z)$, where Z is an imperative.

(g) (Z) o (Y), (Y) o (Z), where Z is an imperative of the form $-(-(X)$ v $(Y))$ and Y is an indicative.

(B) The expressions of the following forms are the only imperatives of N_1^* :

(a) $Z [Y]$, $Z [Y_1, Y_2,...,Y^n]$, as in (A) (a).

(b) $-(Z)$, where Z is an imperative.

(c) $(X) (Z)$, where X is an individual variable and Z is imperative.

(d) (Z) v (Y), where Z and Y are both imperatives.

(e) (Z) o (Y), (Y) o (Z), where Y is an indicative and Z is an imperative not equivalent to any other imperative of the form $-(- (X) v (X))$.

Definitions :

1. $\exists x(Z)=$Def. $-(X)-(Z)$, where Z is an imperative or an indicative, and X is an individual variable.

2. $(Z) \to (Y)=$Def. $-(Z) v (Y)$, where Z and Y are both indicatives or both imperatives.

3. $(Z) \to (Y)=$Def. $-(Z) o (Y)$, where Z in an indicative and Y is an imperative.

4. $(Z).(Y)=$Def. $-(-(Z) v-(Y)$, where Z and Y are both imperatives or both indicatives.

5. $(Z) \& (Y)=$Def. $-(-(Z) o-(Y)$, where Z is an indicative and Y is an imperative.

6. $(Z)\equiv(Y)=$Def. $((Z) \to (Y)).((Y) \to (Z))$, where Z and Y are both indicatives or both imperatives.

(3) Rules for deductive inference in N_1^* :

I. *Modus ponens*

II. *Rule of universalization*

III. *Rule of normative inference :* If Z and Y are imperatives of N_1^* and the indicative $(I (Z)) \to$ (I) (Y) is demonstrable (provable) in N_1^* without the necessity of any of the following propositions :

$(I (ZvI)) \to (I (ZoI (Y)))$, $(I (ZoI (Y))) \to (I (Zvy))$, $((ZvI)) \to (I (I (Z) oY))$, $(I ((Z) oY)) \to (I (ZvY))$, $(I (ZoI (Y)) \to (I ((Z) oY))$. $(I (I (Z) oY)) \to (I (ZoI (Y)))$, then the (normative (indicative $(K(Z)) \to (K(Y))$ is also demonstrable in N_1^*.

(4) *Axioms of N_1^**
The propositions of the following forms are demonstrable in N_1^* :

(1) Axioms of general logic : The version of Paul Barnays in conjunction with that in the *Principia Mathemetica* (of Whitehead and Russell) :

    A1. $ZvZ{\rightarrow}Z$

    A2. $Z{\rightarrow}ZvY$

    A3. $ZvY{\rightarrow}YvZ$ (In these four axioms X, Y, and Z are all indicatives.)

    A4. $(Y{\rightarrow}Z){\rightarrow}(XvY{\rightarrow}XvZ)$

(2) Axioms of quantificational logic : A group of axioms which appear to be due to F.F. Fitch :

    A5. $(X) (Y{\rightarrow}Z){\rightarrow}((X) (Y){\rightarrow}(X) (Z))$

    A6. $Y{\rightarrow}(X) (Y)$, in all cases where the individual constant X is not free in Y, that is, X does not occur in Y, or if it occurs in part Z of Y, such that $(X) (Z)$ is part of Y.

    A7. $(X) (Y){\rightarrow}(Z)$, where Z is equal to Y except in all those instances where the individual variable X is free in Y, the variable T (not necessarily distinct from X) is free in Z, or T is a proper name.

(In these axioms A5.—A7., Y and Z are indicatives, X and T and individual variables.)

(3) Axioms for the imperative logic (or of the indicatives formed with 'I') :

    A8. $I(Z_nX_1, X_2,...,X_n){\equiv}Z_n(X_1X_2,...,X_n)$

    A9. $I(-Z){\equiv}-I(Z)$

    A10. $I(YvZ){\equiv}I(Y)vI (Z)$

    A11. $I(YoZ){\equiv}(Y)vI(Z)$

    A12. $I(ZoY){\equiv}(Z)vY$

    A13. $I((X) (Z){\equiv}(X) (I (Z))$

(In these axioms, A8.=A13., it is supposed that expressions are indicatives or imperatives, following the rules of formation.)

(4) Special axioms of the normative logic (or of the indicatives formed with 'K') : In these axioms X and Y are imperatives, and X is a variable.

A14. $K(Z) \rightarrow -K(-Z)$

(This proposition establishes that if the execution of an act is obligatory, then its non-execution is not obligatory.)

A15. $K(Y.Z) \equiv K(Y). K(Z)$

(A15. says that given that it is obligatory to do two acts, then it is obligatory to do each one of them separately, and vice versa.)

A16. $K(Y\&Z) \equiv Y.K(Z)$

(A16. states that if it is obligatory to do an act Y, and circumstances Z are present only when Y is obligatory, then those circumstances Z are obligatory when Y is done.)

A17. $K(K (Z) \rightarrow Z)$

(This proposition states that it is obligatory to do an obligatory act Z.)

A18. $(X) (K (Z) \rightarrow K (X) (Z))$

(Axiom 18. states that where it is obligatory for all to do Z, then it is obligatory for all to do Z.)

By way of completing the presentation of Castaneda's system, the three ways in which N_1* is extended are enumerated.[138]

"1. The propositional logic is extended, by means of (formulation rule (2) A) (c) and the rule of universalization, and axioms A5. to A7., to functional calculus;

2. The functional logic is extended, by means of the rules of formation of imperatives and (2) (A) (e) and (2) (A) (g) and the axioms A8. to A13., to a logic of imperatives;

3. The logic of imperatives is extended, by means of rules (2) (A) (f) and Rule III and the axioms A14. to A18., to a normative logic."

What is immediately striking about Castaneda's system, as opposed to a system of say Hofstadter and McKinsey, is the greater richness of the former. Castaneda typifies the trend by recent writers who formulate logics of impe-ratives by employing the advances in logic to clarify and precisely illustrate the nature of relations holding between indicatives, imperatives, and norms. For as it has been seen, Castaneda does more than just to introduce a new symbol '!', as was the case with Hofstadter and McKinsey. He is seen to employ new primitives, such as 'o', 'I', and 'K'. Also, he extends the propositional logic his system contains into a functional logic, by means of axioms, and goes further by extending it into a logic of imperatives, and further again into a logic of norms. Thus one sees in Castaneda's work a more sophisticated effort, from a logical point of view, towards presenting a logic of imperatives, than has been the case thus far.

Thus it is proper to consider first the primitives Castaneda introduces, as to what they do and how adequate they are in articulating a new logic of imperatives, and then to go on and consider this logic as a complete system. In view of this, therefore, the primitive 'o' becomes the first point of scrutiny. Castaneda says that 'o' expresses the "mixed disjunction" of an imperative and an indicative. Such a disjunction would be tantamount to : "Either come to see me or the sky is blue." and "The sky is blue or come to see me." The pertinent question here is whether there can be an "intelligible" disjunctive statement, where we have an imperative and an indicative as disjuncts.

It appears that where one has an indicative and an

imperative, and attempts to combine the two by a disjunctive connective (like 'o'), then no meaningful disjunctive statement results. In the examples given above, no meaningful choice-offering relation seems to arise from saying "Either come to see me or the sky is blue." The relation of choice between two distinct alternatives, or the expression of the notion that either one or both of two alternatives are true or false, does not seem to be conveyed by a type of disjunction which requires that one disjunct be an imperative and the other be an indicative. Thus there seems to be a problem as to the adequacy of Castaneda's symbol 'o', in its being able to form intelligible disjunctive statements. Furthermore, the preceding objection does not pertain to the *meaning* of 'o', but rather it is directed to the *function* of 'o' in N_1^*. For to attack the meaning of 'o' would be of no avail, since Castaneda takes 'o' as an *undefined primitive* of N_1^*. On the other hand, to show how one of the primitives of his calculus does not really function as he says it does, undermines the very *basis* of the system presented by Castaneda.

The one way in which an imperative and an indicative can be combined semantically is to consider them in an implicational sense. Thus, for example, the statement "Shut the door *for* it is getting cold." is a case where an imperative and an indicative are intelligibly combined. Similarly the statement "You have your weapons, *therefore* fight !" is a case where the indicative is combined with an imperative, in an implicational sense. One would interpret each of the statements above as saying that the door is to be closed *because* it is cold, and *because* you have your weapons you are to fight. Thus it is seen that in an implicational rather than disjunctive sense, the combination of imperatives with indicatives, and conversely, can be meaningfully brought about. Yet even here, the implication involved must still be explained as logical implication. Thus the problem of assigning truth values to imperatives emerges again.

If what has been said about Castaneda's symbol 'o' is

justified, then the system N_1* is untenable. For the formation rules (2) (A) (g) and (2) (B) (e), articulated by means of
"mixed disjunction" or 'o', must be dropped. Similarly,
definitions 3 and 4 are no longer acceptable, the all-
important Rule of Normative Inference is untenable, and
axioms A. 11 and A. 12 of N_1* must also be reassessed.
Of more far reaching significance is the result that without
formation rules (2) (A) (g) and (2) (B) (e) above, and axioms
A. 11 and A. 12 Castaneda cannot extend his functional
logic to a logic of imperatives. Also, without Rule III he
could not extend his imperative logic (assuming one could
effectively devise such a logic along the lines suggested by
him) to a normative logic. All of the rules and axioms
which are pointed to as being inadequate, involve in some
way the symbol 'o' and are thus open to dispute.

It is notable also that the only review of the system N_1*
by Gerold Stahl in *The Journal of Symbolic Logic* (1957)
finds nothing wrong with the way the symbol 'o' yields
intelligible disjunctive-indicative statements. Stahl accepts
the use of 'o' and comments upon the entire system itself
as being "very suggestive."[139]

Objections can also be raised as to the acceptability of
the symbol 'I' in the system N_1*, with respect to the way
this symbol is said to "refine" the corresponding indicatives
of imperatives and norms. However, because the question
has been raised as to the syntactic nature of this correspondence, the adequacy of 'I' need not be discussed.

Viewing the system N_1* in its totality, however, prompts
the question of whether the logic of imperatives he presents
may be considered separately from his normative logic.
Central to Castaneda's thesis in "A Note on Imperative
Logic" is that he considers the logic of imperatives as
dependent upon the logic of norms. For this reason,
Castaneda terms his logic of imperatives a "semi-logic."
Thus the question poised is whether or not the logic of
imperatives in N_1* can be considered independently of the
logic of norms.

Assuming that the primitive 'o' could be accepted, it does not become apparent why, as Castaneda's central thesis maintains, the logic of imperatives must be *dependent* upon a normative logic, and thus be termed a "semi-logic." For it seems obvious that one can give all the formation rules, definitions, rules of deductive inference (except inference Rule III), axioms A1 to A3, without mentioning anything about normative logic. If anything, it is normative logic which is directly dependent upon a logic of imperatives as his inference Rule III shows.

In "Inference, Decisions, and "Oughts" ", Castaneda's "new" position sees the *differences* between imperatives and norms as follows :

"(1) The causal intention, i.e. the behavior-influencing rule of prescriptive language, is essential to imperatives...

(2) The Characteristic function of normatives as such does not consist in influencing behavior or telling somebody what to do, but in *somehow* relating actions to considerations or grounds for them.

(3) The fundamental function of normatives is intimately connected with the roles of their qualifiers..."[140]

Thus he now sees no direct *dependence* between imperatives and norms, Characteristic (1) is, in short, not in any sense assumed or precluded within characteristics (2) and/or (3), as he believes in "*Una Sistema General de Logica Normativa.*"

In another passage of "Imperatives, Decisions, and "Oughts" " Castaneda attempts to clarify further the relation between imperatives and norms by saying :

"Here I will just dogmatically say that, as I view it, one of the fundamental links between "X ought (unqualifiedly) to do A" and "X, do A" is that the former *expresses, points to*, or obliquely talks about the justifiedness of the latter in the absolute or total context of ends, facts, conventions, and decisions; but it does not assert what these are. Indeed, it does not even assert that the imperative is justified, much

less talk about the justification directly. It merely says in
the object-language, i.e., in the material mode of speech...
what the second-order statement, "The imperative 'X, do
A' is necessarily justified in the absolute context of ends
etc.," says in the meta-language of the language of
action..."[141]

The above passage suggests the autonomy, so to speak,
of imperatives as apart from norms. For the justifiedness
of imperatives, as well as their *assertive* function, is now
not held to be in any way particularly asserted by norms.
It is only in the large absolute sense of such justification
that norms say anything about imperatives, and even here
a norm is said to speak "obliquely" or in a meta-language
of the justification of imperatives. All this again goes to
illustrate the point that contrary to Castaneda's position in
"*Una Sistema General de Logica Normativa*" there is no
discernibly close dependence of imperatives on norms. Yet
it is such a dependence which he maintains in explaining
his system N_1^*, as well as his explanation of how his logic
departs from that of Hare's, in his article "A Note on Imperative Logic."

Apart from the problems which upset Castaneda's
attempt, the system N_1^* illustrates a new technique for
formulating a logic of imperatives. This consists in using
a higher order functional calculus to express logical relations
in imperative and normative logic. Hence he initiates a
trend placing more emphasis upon the use of logic, rather
than upon the power of the intensional analysis of imperatives, to secure a formal systematization of imperatives.
Though Castaneda engages in some intensional analysis,
insofar as he presents the "intuited" characteristics of
norms, imperatives, and descriptive indicatives, he departs
significantly from all other intensionalists in that he seeks
to employ more powerful logic to express the many subtleties imperatives are found to reflect contextually.

Section 2. *Von Wright's 'Denotic Logic of Categorical Norms'*

Von Wright's importance in the study of imperative

logics is primarily that of his being the first to employ modal logic to formulate a logic of norms or imperatives. However he will be considered here in light of his most recent attempts at formulating such a logic. For he takes his position in *Norm and Action* as a refinement upon his earlier views in "Deontic Logic," particularly in that he considers a logic of norms to be possible in his later work without resorting to modal logic. Central to Von Wright's latest attempt is the idea that a deontic logic or a logic of normative propositions can be articulated by means of the basic features of the propositional calculus.[142]

Von Wright divides norms into three groups : "rules," "prescriptions," and "directives." In the first group of "rules" he includes the rules of logic, mathematics, etc. Under prescriptions he includes commands, permissions, and prohibitions which govern an agent's conduct. Finally, under "directives" are included the so-called "technical norms," that is actions which must be done so as to secure certain determinable ends.[143]

Though Von Wright concentrates more upon the development of a logic of prescriptive norms, it is seen that common to all the groups of norms mentioned above is the notion of action of some sort, which plays an important part in the meaning one attaches to each type of norm. Thus as a basis for the Logic of Norms, Von Wright proceeds first to develop a Logic of Action, which is to form the kernel of a Logic of Norms.[144]

Furthermore, Von Wright indicates that fundamental to all kinds of action is the notion of "change" from one state of affairs to another. Thus, the Logic of Action presupposes a Logic of Change, and the development of the latter becomes Von Wright's first concern. More importantly, it is at the level of the Logic of Change that the application of the propositional calculus in the formation of deontic logic (or normative logic) is most readily seen.[145]

Thus the first logic Von Wright deals with assumes some

of the techniques of the propositional logic, such as the construction of truth tables and the transforming of expressions into their *normal form*, that is, the expression of a statement in terms of its disjuncts, each of which is a conjunction of true or false statements.[146]

With this foundation from the calculus of propositions, Von Wright introduces the primitive 'T' as the symbol which describes change. Thus the expression 'pT-p' describes the (generic) event of the transformation from state of affairs p to state of affairs-p. T-expressions by themselves are termed atomic, and where they are combined with other T-expressions will be termed molecular.[147]

The rules governing the use of T-expressions are derived from the fundamental two-valued propositional logic. For there are four *elementary* (state-) *transformations* possible for a given "feature of the world :" pTp, pT-p,-pTp, and -pT-p. These rules are taken as "mutually exclusive" and "*jointly exhaustive.*" Thus, where 'p' means that the door is open, 'pTp' means that the door remains open, 'pT-p' means that the door was open but has been closed, '-pTp' means that the door was closed but is now open, and '-pT-p' means that the door remains closed.[148]

Before passing on to the way Von Wright considers the above state-descriptions as functions of "change-description," it is important to see how he conceives of the role of the "agent" with respect to the "features" of the world mentioned above. Basically, Von Wright conceives of an agent as an empirical agent who is perishable, as opposed to one who has necessary existence (in some unspecified sense). Also in his view an agent performs an "individual" act whether he is an individual agent or a "collective" agent (that is a number of individuals acting to bring about some one thing). To every act performed by an agent there *intrinsically* corresponds a "change," such as is found in the description of the "features" of the world above. In this way, the action of the agent is *tied up* with the notion of "change" as denoted by 'T'. Thus 'T' comes to involve a more complex idea than the mere transition of one state of affairs to another state of affairs. This in turn makes 'T' more difficult to grasp. For if it denotes action *and* intrinsic change, then in cases such as 'pTp' and '-pT-p', where Von Wright admits that no change occurs, one is to conclude that no action occurs as well. Yet Von Wright insists 'T' *always* denotes action by an agent, (even in the above two cases), and therefore 'T' *always* denotes intrinsic change.[149] Thus in cases such as 'pTp' and '-pT-p', where admittedly no change in a state of affairs occurs, the function of the symbol 'T', becomes highly problematic. Does 'T' express action in these cases, or does it not convey the notion action ?

As a result of the ambiguity of the symbol 'T', serious difficulties arise for Von Wright's Logic of Norms generally. For it is now difficult to claim that his Logic of Change can be evolved *independently* from his Logic of Action. Somehow, with his account of the meaning of 'T', it no longer seems possible to speak of a logic of change as *apart* from a logic of action. Thus Von Wright's Logic of Norms does not stand out as a logic composed of a *clear cut* logic of change and a *clear cut* logic of action. Thus also at the very outset Von Wright's attempt appears to founder with the fundamentals of his presentation.

Continuing, Von Wright presents the following table to illustrate how state-descriptions are functions of "*change descriptions*" (i.e. "Conjunction sentences of some n-elementary T-expressions of n different atomic variables.").[150]

p&q	(pTp) & (qTq)
	(pTp) & (qT-q)
	(pT-p) & (qTq)
	(pT-p) & (qT-q)
p&q	(pTp) & (-qT-q)
	(pTp) & (-qTq)
	(pT-p) & (-qT-q)
	(pT-p) & (-qTq)

-p&q	(-pT-p) & (qTq)
	(-pT-p) & (qT-q)
	(pTp) & (qTq)
	(-pTp) & (qT-q)
-p&-q	(-pT-p) & (-qT-q)
	(-pT-p) & (-qTq)
	(-pTp) & (-qT-q)
	(-pTp) & (-qTq)

By way of briefly explicating Von Wright's table it can be said that state-description p&q is *open to change* in one of four following ways : (pTp) & (qTq), which means that p and q do not change; (pTp) & (qT-q), which means that p does not change but q changes; (pT-p) & (qTq) which means that p changes but q does not change; and (pT-p) & (qT-q), which means that p changes and q changes.[151]

Since Von Wright bases his Logic of Categorical Norms on a Logic of Change and a Logic of Action, the strength of his Logic of Norms could be no sounder than the foundation upon which he bases it. Thus a criticism of his Logic of Change is a criticism of the basis of his Logic of Norms.

One immediate difficulty with accepting Von Wright's Logic of Change concerns the way in which T is said to describe "states of affairs." The author does not go very far in explaining what these states are, other than considering them as in some way synonymous with "features of the world." It is important to point out here the vagueness of this apparently crucial notion in Von Wright's position. For if he cannot be explicit in saying just what it is that 'T' is descriptive of, then the cornerstone of his Logic of Norms seems to be unable to support the structure he intends to build upon it. Yet it is evident from a careful reading that the expression "states of affairs" is not elucidated by the author. There is very little suggested as to what constitutes a world or a feature of a world in the expression "features of the world," which is taken as in some way explaining what a "state of affairs" involves.

Von Wright's conception of "transition" is also difficult to grasp in view of his remarks in the introduction to *Norm and Action*. For at the very outset he says that propositional logic deals with the *static* world of true and false propositions.[152] By this he means that propositional logic does not express anything about the *Changing* of statements *from* true *to* false. Rather it relates by means of connectives definitely determined proposition, insofar as the latter form elemental parts of new propositions. In this way the propositional calculus says nothing about the modality of action. However, it is recalled that Von Wright bases his Logic of Change upon the two-valued propositional logic. This is seen in the way he presents the four possible states of affairs which manifest transition, that is, pTp, pT-p, -pTp, and -pT-p. Thus one is left with the alternative of interpreting the expression 'pT-p', for example as a description of the transition from the static state of affairs p to static state of affairs-p. If this is what the author means for 'T' to describe, then again it is difficult to see how 'T' describes a transition. Thus the problem of just *how* one can have a transition from one static state of affairs to another static state of affairs is difficult to circumvent.

Before sketching Von Wright's Logic of Action, which forms the second level of his Logic of Categorical Norms, it is important to consider some new symbolism, as well as his presentation of the "eight elementary acts and forbearances."

The new symbol Von Wright introduces is 'd', which is to stand for the agent's action. Hence, incorporating the Logic of Change, 'd(pTp), is a schematic representation of a sentence which expresses the act of "preserving p," where p is state of affairs obtaining prior to any action by a particular agent. In a similar manner 'd(pT-p)' describes the agent's act of "destroying p," where p is a state of affairs obtaining prior to the agent's action. Also, 'd-(-pTp)' describes the "doing of p," where the state of affairs -p obtains prior to action. Finally, the schema 'd(-pT-p)' describes the act of the "suppression of p," where -p obtains prior to action.[153]

One would fail to grasp the role of 'd' in sentences if something more is not said on how Von Wright conceives of propositions. For in his view 'd(pTp), is a schematic representation of a sentence which expresses a "generic proposition." The latter is a proposition which does not have a truth-value by itself, but becomes true or false only when it is instantiated in an individual proposition. Thus an expression such as 'd(pTp)' is a schematization of a sentence expressing the agent's action to effect the "generic" event pTp.[154]

However, a conflict appears to arise between the meaning of 'T' and the meaning of 'd'. For it has been seen that Von Wright considers 'T' as meaning not only transition but also intrinsic action by an agent. Yet he also introduces the symbol 'd' to stand for the agent's action in bringing about a "feature of the world" (or generic event). Thus in order to avoid the confusion of having two symbols standing for an agent's action, he must either drop that sense of 'T', which involves the agent's action, or he must distinguish between the action referred to by 'T'; from the action meant by 'd'. The former alternative involves considering transition as somehow distinct from action. This is an outcome which Von Wright carefully seeks to avoid. On the other hand, the second alternative involves looking upon the action expressed by 'T' as action which has already occurred, whereas the action involved by 'd' is action being performed by the agent. However, Von Wright does not clarify how action is to be taken in 'd' and in 'T'. Thus the above distinctions run the risk of reading too much into Von Wright's presentation.

As "correlatives" of acts, Von Wright conceives of "forbearances," which are symbolized by 'f'. Forbearances, however, are said to be different from the act of "not doing." For forbearances cannot be defined in terms of actions or changes alone. Von Wright attempts to define "forbearance" as "the doing of a certain thing, if, and only if, he *can do* this thing, but does in fact *not do* it."[155]

In terms of the above so-called "correlatives" of acts, he proceeds to give the following schemata. First, he takes 'f(-pTp)' as the *"forbearing to do"* where '-p' is the state of affairs obtaining before the forbearing, *and* -p does not of itself change to p. Secondly, 'f(pT-p)' means that one *"forbears to destroy"* the state described by 'p'. Again the latter forbearance is possible only because p does not of *itself* change into -p. Thirdly, 'f(pTp)' means that one "forbears to preserve" the state described by 'p', where p will change to -p, "unless the change is prevented through an agent's action." Finally, "...f '(-pT-p)' means that one forbears to suppress the state of affairs described by '-p'." The latter holds where, on the occasion in question, the -p state of affairs will change into the p state of affairs, "unless the change is prevented through action."[156]

Whereas 'd-expressions' describing actions seem to relate more concretely to the bringing about of the "four" features of the world,' there is a certain vagueness about Von Wright's view that forbearances are correlates of acts or 'd-expressions,' and thus that forbearances are somehow involved in action. However, out of fairness to Von Wright the following table relating acts, forbearances, and changes is presented, after which a criticism of his notion of "forbearance" will be given.[157]

Condition of Action	Act or forbearances	Result of action
pT-p p is but vanishes, unless preserved	d(pTp) p is preserved	pTp p remains
same	f(pTp) one lets p vanish	pT-p p vanishes
pTp p is and remains, unless destroyed	d(pT-p) p is destroyed	pT-p p vanishes
same	f(pT-p) one lets p remain	pT-p p remains

-pT-p	d(-pTp)	-pTp
p is not and does not happen, unless produced	p is produced	p happens
same	f(-pTp) one lets p remain absent	-pT-p p remains absent

-pTp	d(-pT-p)	-pT-p
p is not but happens, unless suppressed	p is suppressed	p remains absent
same	f(-pT-p) one lets p happen	-pTp p happens

Before continuing with Von Wright's Logic of Action it is constructive to see how adequate his notion of 'forbearance' is. The simplest way of doing this is to compare the idea of 'forbearance' with his notion of action or of "d-expressions," which he takes to be the correlates of "f-expressions." Von Wright stresses that forbearance is a notion which does not imply any actual action, but rather involves the description of non-action where one could act. This kind of nonaction is distinguished from cases in which one actually suppresses p or -p, the latter Von Writht includes under cases of preservative d-expressions.

Yet it appears that the notion of 'forbearances,' as presented by Von Wright, does not lend itself to the four rules of formation, as is the case with d-expressions. For to forbear to do is really to forbear to do in the *same* way in *every* possible situation in which one forbears to do. One does not seem to do anything essentially different if he forbears to do pT-p, pTp, or -pTp. In all of these cases the result is the same, namely, the "change" (insofar as one assumes the adequacy of Von Wright's account of 'T') bringing about the different state of affairs is not interfered with. The reason for this is that 'forbearance' is not an action, but a *disposition* towards not bringing an action about. On Von

Wright's own terms, there appears to be a basis for saying that forbearances are generically different from acts, in that forbearances do not interfere with states of affairs.

Thus as dispositions toward not acting, forbearances cannot but reflect the context in which they operate. Put in clearer terms, the apparent difference in forbearing pT-p and -pTp arises not from the disposition of *forbearing itself*, but from the context or meaning of the circumstance, in this case, pT-p, pTp, -pTp, etc. It makes no more sense to say that one can positively, or indifferently forbear, than it is to say that one can be positively, negatively or indifferently pleased. Here, as in the case of forbearance, it is only the context which can explain what it means to be pleased in any one of the three ways mentioned. Therefore, to be pleased is to be disposed in some way towards an object, just as to forbear is to be disposed towards not interfering in some particular situation. Yet to explain how one is disposed to forbear, for example, in a particular case requires that the case itself be considered.

If this analysis of Von Wright's notion of forbearance is not mistaken, then it is hard to see how forbearances can be held as "correlates" of action. Essentially, it is seen that there is really *only one* state of forbearance, which is a disposition, and which is present in differing contexts. Action, however, is taken by Von Wright in a behavioral sense. Thus he says that d(-pTp) is the *doing of* p, (-pTp) is *the suppression of* p, etc., and these are *distinct* actions in his behavioral sense. Thus the question arises as to how forbearance itself can be taken as a correlate of a number of distinct actions. It seems that Von Wright is comparing two different types of things, namely acts and forbearance. Acts are not dispositions since in Von Wright's sense to act is to interfere with a state of affairs. Thus what is being asked here is at least the intimation of the problem of *how* forbearance and actions can be related. In reading Von Wright on this score, however, one assumes that forbearance is self-evidently the correlate of acts. This does not seem evident however.

In spite of the above problem a brief account of Von

Wright's Logic of Action can be presented. Here he is seen to present a new expression : 'df', which is an atomic d- and an atomic f-expression, or molecular complexes of atomic d- and/or atomic f-expressions. Thus, for example, "d(pTp) & f (-qTq) is a df-expression." Furthermore, the logic of df-expressions is held to be part of a (general) Logic of Action.[158]

Von Wright goes on to state that elementary acts and elementary forbearances are *mutually exculsive* on three accounts. First, a person cannot act and forbear at the same time. Secondly, two of the four types of acts discussed above are mutually exclusive, with respect to a given state of affairs. This can be seen in the case of d(pTp) and d(-pTp). For both, of these acts cannot be done at the same time, nor, from the point of view of what these expressions describe, can both these cases come about at the same time. Thirdly, it follows that two of the four types of forbearances, which, like the above two acts, are also mutually exclusive. For one cannot forbear to preserve p and forbear to suppress p at one and the same time. Furthermore, Von Wright concludes that all eight elementary acts and forbearances are mutually exclusive of each other.[159]

In a telling passage Von Wright goes on to explain the essential condition which is to underline his presentation of the Logic of Action :

> "Only on condition that the agent *can* produce and suppress and destroy *and* preserve a given state of affairs, is it the case that he necessarily will, on any given occasion, either produce or forbear producing, suppress *or* forbear suppressing, destroy *or* forbear destroying, *or* preserve *or* forbear preserving this state of affairs."[160]

Pursuing the Logic of Action, Von Wright goes on to present the truth-function of df-expressions. The distributive properties of d-and f-expressions are axiomatic to the df-calculus, and hence cannot be proved within this calculus itself. However, Von Wright believes that the "intuitive plausibility" of these properties is evident from the examples which follow.[161]

He begins by taking an atomic d-expression, whose T-expression is put in a positive normal form, that is, the T-expression is put into a disjunction of conjunctions of elementary T-expressions. The conjunctions of the normal form of T describe "mutually exclusive ways in which the world changes and/or remains unchanged." Here Von Wright notes that the d-operator is disjunctively distributive in front of T-expressions. Thus in the case of d(-pTp v (pT-p), one can also say without ambiguity that d(-pTp) v d(pT-p). Because of the distributive quality of d-expressions every atomic d-expressions can be replaced by a disjunction of d-expressions, in which the d-operator stands in front of a change description." Thus the same distribution occurs with an expression such as 'd((pT-p) & (qT-q))'.[162]

Von Wright illustrates how f-expressions are also disjunctively distributive. He states that where there are two mutually exclusive changes, meaning that an individual forbears one thing or another, that is, he does neither one thing nor another, the f-operator disjunctively distributes in front of the perfect normal form of T-expressions. Thus 'f((-pTp) v (pT-p))' means the same as f(-pTp) v f(-pTp). Also, in the case of change-descriptions, Von Wright states that the f-operator, like the d-operator, is disjunctively distributed. Hence the statement f((pT-p) & (qT-q)) is equal to f(pT-p) v f(qT-q).[163]

According to Von Wright, truth tables can be constructed to investigate the truth-function of df-expressions. Such a procedure would see the tables governed by the limitations of the joint exhaustiveness and mutual exclusiveness of the eight elementary acts and forbearances with respect to a given state of affairs. Where a df-expression is a tautology, its truth-function shall be determined as true by d- and f-expressions. Thus one would say that a df-expression is a tautology because its constituents (the elementary d- and f-expressions which make up the df-expressions) yield a tautology. In an analogous way, the contradiction of the df-constituents will be termed the df-contradiction. Examples of df-tautology and df-contradiction are : -d(pTp) v -f(pTp) and d(pTp) & f(pTp) respectively.[164]

An account of Von Wright's Logic of Action would be incomplete if something were not said about the way in which df-expressions have a "*positive normal form.*" For it is only the positive normal form of df-expressions which he considers as the proper form for df-expressions. By "positive normal form" of df-expressions Von Wright means the disjunction sentence of conjunctive sentences of elementary d-and/or f-expressions, which contain no negation sentences of elementary d-and/or f-expressions.[165]

The positive normal form of df-expressions is arrived at by first transforming the df-expression into a molecular complex of d- and or f-expressions. The resulting expression of the df-expression in turn is transformed into its own perfect disjunctive normal form. The latter "is a conjunction-sentence of conjunction-sentences of elementary d- and/or f-expressions and/or negation-sentences of elementary expressions." Furthermore, all negation-sentences of the above normal form shall be replaced by a 7-termed disjunctive-sentence of elementary expressions. With this latter move the df-expression is finally put in its positive disjunctive normal form.[166]

Because the account of Von Wright's Logic of Action is meant to be only a summary of his view, the expounding of his illustration of just how the perfect normal form of df-expression is arrived at shall be deferred. It is enough to point out, however, that the simple illustration Von Wright presents ends up being an expression showing fifteen mutually exclusive generic modes of action, which are all included in the most simple case of d(pTp) v d (qTq). Thus the enormous complexity of his Logic of Action is most evident.[167]

By way of rounding out the conceptual framework in which the Logic of Action is said to be operative, the motion of "act-description" is defined by Von Wright as "a conjunction-sentence of some n elementary d- and/or f-expressions of n different atomic variables." Hence d(pTp) & f(qT-q) is an act-description. With this notion one is projected to the groundwork of his Logic of Norms. For essential to this latter logic is the idea that in prohibiting or in considering something as obligatory one calls forth that some "act-description" be satisfied by an agent. Thus is seen the interconnection of the Logic of Action within the Logic of Norms.[168]

However, without entering into the Logic of Norms, it can be contested that Von Wright has backed away from his primary aim of presenting a logic of *prescriptive* (i.e. imperative) discourse, and attempts instead to formulate a logic which is *descriptive* of prescriptive discourse. Furthermore, it will be found that Von Wright's attempt at glossing over these two distinct approaches to a logic of normative propositions is not convincing, and that his Logic of Norms is open to the charge that it does not concern itself with a logic of prescriptive proposition at all.

Von Wright argues for his Logic of Norms by saying that the connectives 'or', 'and', etc. of the propositional calculus cannot be used for forming molecular expression of O-expressions, which are obligatory propositions. Nor can these connectives be used for forming molecular expressions of P-expressions, which are permissive norms. Thus Von Wright adds that though his Logic of Norms deals only with the descriptive interpretation of O-and P-expressions, he finds the rules of this logic reflective of the "logical properties" (sense unspecified) of unaltered prescriptive proposistions. "Thus, in a sense, the 'basis' of Deontic Logic (that is the logic of O- and P-expressions) is a theory of prescriptive discourse."[169]

However, his announced aim of interpreting 'O' descriptively renders everything one has to say about norms in his Logic of Norms metalinguistic, in the sense that this logic can only deal with statements about norms, but never with

norms in their full unaltered *prescriptive* sense. It is un-
fortunate that Von Wright does not elect to discuss the
nature of the relation between a "norm-formulation" and
a norm. In an unduly vague passage he only says that
norm-formulation relate to norms in a "performative"
sense. Here, however, so brief are his remarks that no
meaningful position can be gleaned as to the nature of the
indicated relation.[170]

Von Wright also says that : "one must not break one's
head over the question whether 'and' means the same thing
or not..." in a descriptive or a prescriptive sentence concerning the same subject matter. For only in the descriptive
sentence is there the expression of a truth-function, while
there is no truth-function expressed with 'and' in the prescriptive sentence. Thus Von Wright is saying that one is
forever stopped from formulating a logic in which norms
(or imperatives) *qua* norms (or imperatives) can be inferred
from other norms.[171] In his view the best that can be done
is to translate or "interpret" imperatives into some sort of
descriptive propositions, with the aid of the above mentioned logic.

What Von Wright's attempt come down to, apart from
the refinements of considering the Logic of Change and the
Logic of Action, is a logic similar to that of Hofstadter and
McKinsey. For by his Logic of Norms he translates a norm
or imperative into something non-prescriptive or non-imperative, and the latter in some unspecified sense "accom-
modates" a norm in a two-valued propositional logic.

Here again, as with the other attempts thus far considered, the crucial question of whether a logic which transforms imperatives into descriptive indicatives can be
accepted as an adequate logic for accounting for imperative
reasoning arises. As before, the problem of the means by
which the imperative mood of the imperative is to be handled remains.

Thus without going very far into Von Wright's logic of
Norms, it is evident that we are not dealing with a logic of

norms *qua* norms. Thus in spite of his insistence that the rules of his Logic of Norms reflect the "logical properties" of norm propositions, it cannot be said that his logic deals with norms in a prescriptive sense. Rather it deals with statements *about* norms in a descriptive and thus nonnormative sense.

However, in his denial that a logic dealing with prescriptive propositions is possible, Von Wright is departing from those who formulated a logic of imperatives in terms of indicatives and considered it *the same as* a logic dealing with prescriptive propositions. For whereas the positivists arrived at the conclusion of the impossibility of a logic of prescriptive statements on account of the meaninglessness of imperatives, Von Wright arrives at this same conclusion on different grounds. As has been seen, he decides to develop the Logic of Norms because he finds the *meaning* of prescriptive propositions (sentences) unsuited for formulation in a two-valued propositional logic. Thus he holds norms or imperatives generally to be meaningful, contrary to the positivists' outlook. Furthermore, he at least recognizes the difference between a logic of descriptive propositions *about* norms, and a logic of prescriptive propositions. There is no suggestion on Von Wright's part that the former logic, if possible, would be identical to the latter logic. Thus Von Wright avoids the reduction of the former to the latter as the positivists maintained.

Therefore, with Von Wright's admission that a logic of prescriptive propositions is impossible, the intensionalists' approach has arrived to the point of saying that the best which can be done is to develop a logic of imperatives, involving propositions which are descriptive of imperatives or norms. The most recent discussions of the problem have therefore attempted to make such a logic more acceptable by either developing the conceptual framework of this logic, or by employing still more advanced techniques of logic than Von Wright's to enhance the power of such a logic. From this perspective the contributions of N. Rescher are considered.

Section 3 : *Rescher's Logic of Commands*

In his introduction to *The Logic of Commands* Nicholas Rescher sees the "key" problem permeating the major attempts at formulating logics of imperatives as that of incorporating imperatives within a two-valued propositional calculus. Thus he gears his entire outlook to account for such reasoning, and it is from this point of view that his contributions will be considered.[172]

In the seventh chapter of *The Logic of Commands* Rescher attempts to come to grips with the nature of "imperative validity." To do this he explains "command inference" as "an argument whose conclusion is a command, and whose premises include commands and possibly also assertoric statements." The problem of central importance is determining the "conditions and circumstances under which an 'inference' involving commands is to count as valid..."[173]

Rescher proceeds to explain imperative validity in command inference as analogous to ordinary indicative inference of the type :

> "All felines are mammals.
> All lions are felines.
> _____
> All lions are mammals."

Thus he claims that just as the conclusion of the above inference is implicitly asserted or accepted by anyone overtly asserting the premises of this inference, so also where an inference involving commands is the case, the conclusion follows as above. Hence in the example :

> "Always say 'please' to John when you ask him
>   for the bread ! !
> Ask John for the bread now !
> _____
> Say 'please' to John now ! "

the conclusion is seen to follow validly from the premises of the syllogism in the sense that the "conclusion is tacitly or implicitly contained in its premisses..." Three conditions appear to be involved in the valid inferring of commands :

"(i)   *Anyone* who overtly *gives* the premiss commands may legitimately claim (or be claimed) to have implicitly given the command conclusion. ‑

(ii)   *Anyone* who overtly *receives* the premiss commands may legitimately claim (or be claimed) to have implicitly received the command conclusion.

(iii) Any course of action on the part of their common recipient which terminates the premiss commands cannot fail to terminate the command conclusion."

In view of condition (iii), Rescher proceeds to a "rule of rejection" for doing away with some kinds of command inferences. This rule simply states that a command inference is invalid if the indicative and/or command premisses of the imperative syllogism are either true or (in the case of command premisses) terminated, though the command conclusion is unterminated.[174]

In passing it is important to note that Rescher is assuming in his account of imperative inference thus far that imperative inference *is* analogous to indicative inference. Rescher is careful to distinguish between attributing indicative validity to command inferences, and attributing truth-values to commands. For he specifically denies attributing to commands, when taken as premisses or conclusions, truth or falsehood. He refers to imperatives as *terminated*, rather than as true, when imperatives are successfully acted upon. Thus his assumption, with regard to indicatives, is only that imperative inference is analogous to indicative inference.[175]

However, his assumption about the analogous nature of imperative inference tends to reduce command premisses and conclusions to true indicatives. That this is the case follows from the simple observation that if *sound* imperative validity is analogous to *sound* indicative validity, and the latter type of validity deals solely with true indicatives, then the command premises and conclusion are in some sense indicatively true as well. Yet Rescher denies that he is attributing truth to such premises and conclusions. His denial thus makes problematic the way in which indicative validity is analogous to *sound* imperative validity.

Prior to going on to Rescher's general theory of valid command inference some introductory remarks on the central notion of command *coverage* and *decomposition* are in order. In his sense a command C_1 is said to "cover" another command C_2 if the following three conditions are satisfied : "(1) the group of addresses of C_1 includes all of those of C_2; (2) C_1 calls for realizing (doing), though possibly requiring for something additional thereto; and (3) every time at the condition under which C_2 becomes operative is also a time at and condition under which C_1 becomes operative."[176]

Command decomposition is said by Rescher to occur in three steps. These run as follows :[177]

"(1) **Addressee Decomposition**

The command $C=[Y \, ! \, A/P]$ (which says, "Y do A whenever P obtains !") will be *addressee-decomposed*, (*A-decomposed*, for short) into the pair of commands $C_1=[Y_1 \, ! \, A_1/P_1]$ and $C_1=[Y_2 \, ! \, A_2/P_2]$ if the following three conditions are all satisfied :

(i) $Y=Y_1 \cup Y_2$ (which means that Y is both person Y_1 and Y_2)

(ii) $A=A_1=A_2$ (where $A_1=A_2$ stands for A_1 included in A_2 and A_2 is included in A_1 : $(A_1 < A_2)$ and $(A_2 < A_1)$)

(iii) $P \leftrightarrow P_1 \leftrightarrow P_2$ (which means that *execution precondition* P is logically equivalent to execution precondition P_1, and P_1 is equivalent to execution precondition P_2, which is also equivalent to P.)

(2) Requirement Decomposition

The command $C=[Y ! A/P]$ will be said to be *require-ment-decomposed* (R-*decomposed* for short) into the pair of commands $C_1=[Y_1 ! A_1/P_1]$ are $C_2=[Y_2 ! A_2/P_2]$ if the following three conditions are all satisfied :

(i) $Y=Y_1=Y_2$

(ii) $A=(A_1=A_2)$

(iii) $P \leftrightarrow P_1 \leftrightarrow P_2$

(3) Precondition Decomposition

The command $C=[Y ! A/P]$ will be said to be *precon-dition-decomposed* (P-*decomposed* for short) into the pair of commands $C_1=[Y_1 ! A_1/P_1]$ and $C_2=[Y_2 !A_2/P_2]$ if the following three conditions are all satisfied :

(i) $Y=Y_1=Y_2$

(ii) $A=A_1=A_2$

(iii) $P \leftrightarrow (P_1 \ v \ P_2)$"

Rescher observes that a command covers "every command that figures in its decomposition."

Returning to his general theory of command inference, Rescher sets down the following condition for *patent vali-dity :*

"The inference whose conclusion is the command C and whose premisses include the commands $C_1 \ C_2, ..., C_n$ is *patently valid* if the command C can be decomposed into the set of commands $C_1 \# \#$, $C_2 \# \#,..., C_n \# \#$ in such a way that each $C_i \# \#$, is covered by some of the C_i."[178] (The symbol '$\# \#$' expresses the number of commands in set C_1, etc.)

By way of example the following case :

"C_1=John, do A and B (always) ! !

C_2=John, do both C and D whenever P ! !

C_2=John, do both A and C whenever P ! !"

The above is a valid inference since C_3 can be decomposed into the pair :

"C_4=John ! ! A/P

C_5=John ! C/P"

It is seen that C_4 is covered by premiss C_1, and C_5 is covered by premiss C_2.[179]

Enough has been said about Rescher's conception of imperative reasoning to allow for a critical review of his position. The most difficult thing about his account of such reasoning is what he means by the "implicit" containment of a command conclusion within the premisses of an imperative inference. Obviously he intends this containment as analogous to containment in the sense that an indicative is somehow assumed in the meaning of another indicative statement. At least this seems to be implied by his allusion to the syllogism of all lions being mammals. Also, it is seen in the conditions under which *patent validity* is presented, the way in which an imperative conclusion is said to be "implicit" in its premisses is illustrated by his notions of command "coverage" and command "decomposition." In short, Rescher claims that if it can be shown that an imperative conclusion is decomposable into what the premisses of the inference mean, then that conclusion may be said to follow validly from these premisses.

In spite of the introduction of "coverage" and "decomposition", Rescher's account of imperative inference, and therefore of imperative validity, appears to be open to the same type of objections as were poised against R.M. Hare by Peters and others. For it seems that essential to his view is the idea that imperatives are somewhat like indicatives in that they can be shown to imply a variety of different things. Thus all one has to do is put two related imperatives together, and proceed to *draw* a conclusion from them, which is an imperative. Surely this reminds one of the way in which Hare supposed that imperative conclusions were implied or "implicit" within the description which the imperative premisses of a syllogism somehow reflect. Thus the tangent point common to Hare and Rescher is the way both believe that imperative premisses are reducible to other statements, which come to make up the inferred imperative conclusion.

Of course Rescher's means of explaining the nature of the "implicitness" of the conclusion within imperative premisses is more involved than Hare's. Yet the explanation given in terms of command coverage and command decomposition is really no more successful than Hare's less complex account. For Rescher does not escape the charge of reducing command to indicatives. For example, where he shows his conception of "patent validity," he says that each of the premisses of the syllogism :

"C_1 = John, do A and B (always) ! !

C_2 = John, do both C and D whenever P ! !

_____

C_3 = John, do both A and C whenever P ! ! "

are reducible to "C_4 = John ! A/P" and "C_5 = John ! C/P".[180] However, he does not consider how the condition "always" of C_1 assimilates condition P of C_2. If he were to do this, then he must introduce an indicative statement among the premisses which states that all the conditions of P are conditions of "always." This new premiss will serve to connect C_3 with C_1 and C_2, and thus make C_3 an intelligibly inferred *statement*. It is noted also that C_3 a statement of an indicative nature, and not a command. For, as Peters observes in reviewing Hare's position, a command ordinarily presupposes an individual who directs by means of a specified linguistic form another individual who is to act upon the former's directive. In the case of C_3, however, the one making the inference to the command conclusion is most likely the agent himself, and this makes it difficult to accept C_3 as a command, having the same force as the commands in the imperative premisses. Thus it is difficult to see how C_3 can be anything else than an indicative statement if it is to follow validly (in any normally intelligible sense) from its premisses.

The gist of this criticism, therefore, is that even with his explanation of command coverage and command decomposition Rescher has not escaped saying that in order for the above syllogism to be valid it must be interpreted in the indicative mode of speech. In fact, there seems no other way by which one can consider employing his notions of "coverage" and "decomposition" except if the premisses of his syllogism are indicatively interpreted, with regard to how they can be "decomposed" into C_4 and C_5, for example. However, if such an interpretation were allowed, then the clarity of the indicative premisses and conclusion would dispel the aureole of mystery which Rescher believes to lie between the conclusion and the premisses of imperative inferences, and which he thinks is nonindicatively accounted for by the two notions he introduces.

What is surprising about Rescher's attempt is that he accepts the fact that the only plausible interpretation of his logic of commands is to reduce the premisses and conclusions of imperative inferences to indicatives. He finds this the only means whereby a logic of commands is possible, and for this reason his attempt is admittedly akin to that of Jörgensen's, though more use is made of recent logical techniques than is found in Jörgensen's work.[181]

Furthermore, Rescher appears to be mistaken where he says that like Jörgensen he bases his logic of commands on the interrelations of assertoric counterparts of commands, and not upon the 'truth' and 'falsity' of commands. For he summarily dispenses with Ross' account of Jörgensen's position as "unsympathetic," without considering how Ross' study distinguishes between imperative truth and falsity, and imperative "validity."[182] As was pointed out, Ross rightly indicates that Jörgensen and others confuse the truth of imperatives, insofar as they are satisfiable, with the validity of imperatives, insofar as imperatives are inferrable from other imperatives. A careful review of Rescher's account of "patent validity" shows that he is saying that an imperative is validly inferred from other imperatives, *if* it can be shown that the imperative premisses are decomposable into other imperatives : and these latter are the basis of the imperative conclusion *if* the former imperative premisses are satisfied. Is this not accounting for imperative inference by means of the *satisfaction* of imperatives ? It seems that Rescher is actually confusing validity and truth in the same way Jörgensen does.

Rescher specifically intends his presentation of patent validity as a rebuttal to B.A.O. Williams' position that there is no such thing as an imperative inference.[183] As is seen, Rescher believes that once the proper decomposition of premisses expressing imperatives has been performed, then the truth of saying that the overt receiving of command premisses includes the receiving of command conclusions becomes most evident. Williams' position, however, to which attention is now given, seems able to withstand Rescher's onslaught, and has also become a source of controversy for some recent commentators.

In brief Williams argues that the truth-functional schema :
"(D1) p or q; not p; so q"
is not the analogue of the supposed imperative inference:
"(D2) do x or do y; do not do x; so do y."
He notes that those who have attempted to formulate logics of imperatives have maintained, in one way or another, that the above analogy is self-evident, and that all one has to do is to replace the sentential variables of the ordinary propositional calculus with variables ranging over imperatives, and the logic of imperatives is complete. However, (D1) and (D2) are not analogous for the simple reason that since (D2) is a command inference schema, the expression "do x or do y" presents a "choice-offering" situation where x or y are "permitted." This expression, itself, does not say that the joint performance of x and y are permitted. However the second premiss, "do not do x," has the force of *withdrawing* the first premiss of (D2), as if the speaker were changing his mind. Thus the two premisses of (D2) are inconsistent, whereas this is not the case for schema (D1).[184]

In an earlier article, "Can One Infer Commands From Commands ?" N. Rescher and J. Robinson argue that Williams cannot make the sweeping claim that from the one case of the disjunction of commands no logic of imperatives at all possible.[185] In this they are partly supported by Andre Gombay, who in "Imperative Inference and Disjunction," cautions against the oversimplification of the limited conclusion reached by Williams. In an incisive passage Gombay seeks to further clarify the sense in which the premises of (D2) are inconsistent :

> "... logical relations between commands are a function not only of obedience-conditions but also of considerations of *being-in-force;* and where more than one command is given from source to recipient, we are inclined to hold that each command comes into force sequentially, that is only after obedience, or at least a decision about obedience, to the earlier command has taken place..."[186]

It is interesting to see how even with the most recent contributions of Rescher, the question of the acceptability of a logic of imperatives as a logic is *still* very much discussed. Williams' belief that there is no imperative reasoning as such, and that all of what has been considered as a logic of imperative sentences is really an appeal to the "context" of these sentences, causes just as much concern with Rescher as it did with "Jörgensen and Dubislav.

Thus in recent times the contextual analysis of imperatives has evolved into the difficult position of performing more complex studies of imperative sentences, with the use of advanced logical techniques, so as to account for the logic of imperatives. Implicit in the attempts of Castaneda, Von Wright, and Rescher is the idea that ordinary discourse somehow contains such a logic, and that all which has to be done is to perform a sufficiently penetrating analysis with logical tools so as to extract this logic. Yet the end result of their attempts is that they advance no farther than previous investigators in capturing a logic of imperatives. All seem unable to cope with the apparently unyielding issue of how imperative proposition are to be articulated in a two-valued propositional logic. This was seen to be the case with Castaneda who posited the dubious primitive 'o', which was employed so as to combine indicatives and imperatives in the system N_1*. Similarly, Von Wright attempted to capture the logic of prescriptive propositions by means a two-level logic. Yet it was also seen that Von Wright comes around to saying that a logic of prescriptive propositions is not possible, and that the best which can be done is to formulate a logic which is descriptive of normative propositions. Moreover, Rescher seeks to account for the logic of commands (imperatives) by introducing the notions of command "coverage" and "decomposition," but grants that all of what he presents assumes the analysis of Jörgensen, with respect to the latter's belief that a logic of imperatives is possible only by means of reducing imperatives to assertoric statements.

One must be careful, however, not to dismiss the intensional approach of the analysis of imperatives because of the shortcomings of the above people. To do this would be tantamount to making the unjustified claim of Williams. Rather it seems more prudent to say that as of yet no fully successful logic of imperatives has been formulated from an intensionalists' viewpoint. This at least allows for the legitimacy of the intensionalists' approach which should not be jeopardized because of the failure of some to use it successfully.

Section 4. : *Herbert Simon's Logic of Heuristic Decision Making.*

A new turn in the quest for a logic of imperatives, through the use of contextual analysis, has recently been suggested by Herbert Simon. Simon argues that such a logic can be secured by examining how computers handle commands, and employing the mechanical model to explain command communication involving humans.

Herbert A. Simon proposes in three works : "The Logic of Rational Decision," "The Logic of Heuristic Decision

Making," and *The Sciences of the Artificial* that a data processing system or managerial science can serve as a model with which to characterize the logic of human decisions in actions which fulfil imperatives..[187] The advantage of this is said to be twofold. First, by showing that the model's decision making activity parallels that of the human organism's one has a *precise* conceptual framework by which to analyse human decision making. More importantly, a processing system handles imperatives (supposedly) through rules of correspondence, in that imperatives are said to express some existential state within the system. Hence there is no need for developing a special *modal logic* for imperatival discourse, since imperatives can be converted to declaratives, as is the procedure in computers. Thus an imperatival logic is expressable in a two valued propositional logic.[188]

Simon's thesis posits a similarity between the intentional response to a command and the mechanical motion of a computer. What follows shows there is nothing to support this similarity, and that in fact human responses and mechanical movements are not conceptually alike so as to allow for a common context of discourse which applies to both. Moreover, Simon's own calculus of imperatives is found to deal only with indicatives and not with imperatives. Hence his attempt to derive a logic of imperatives within the calculus of propositions involves a distortion of the imperative as a distinct grammatical entity.

Prior to presenting his logic imperatives, Simon offers a number of arguments to support his general contention that human response behavior and mechanical designing are onomastically parallel. In this section these arguments will be examined as they merge into a body of argumentation supporting the mechanistic nature of human response.

According to Simon, accounting for the human behavioral system is not ponderous if that system is viewed as a simple reactor to a complex outer environment. Essentially, the explanation of why one reacts in such and such a way involves considering the environment which triggers the observed action by the agent. Hence, one need not take into account physiological processes so as to explain human behavior, but only the externally observable influences upon the organism and its equally observable reaction to them. This way of looking at human response behavior makes possible its description in terms of a mechanical problem solving activity. The latter constitutes the real essence of what occurs where one responds to a command. Hence mechanical problem solving as exemplified by computers or specified through directives in applied economics, becomes the ideal model with which to account for successful human reaction to a conveyed command in everyday circumstances.[189]

Simon endeavors to show the correspondence between mind and machine by observing how the brain goes through an inventory process in selecting the appropriate response to a command. This survey activity he likens to the computer's review of its bank of responses so as to select the one which will satisfy the request made of it. Moreover, he considers the mind's decision to attend to some specific area of experience, in choosing a response, as again indicative of the self-orientating operation performed by computers. Hence, the very mental factorization of pertinent information, relative to the command and the immediate environment of response, is describable in terms of a mechanical decision making model.[190]

In comparing organism to machine Simon sees no difference between the *addressable* storage of data only machines are capable of, and the mind's own *associative* storage of experience.[191] In the former case, the data entered into the machine must itself be encoded in such a way that it will be available for a suitably encoded request. Hence data is retrievable *because* at the outset it is put in terms which enables the machine to locate it. Human reflection, however, insofar as it is understood, does not encode experiences in its storing activity. Rather, recall takes place on account of the unlimited associations the mind makes through its encounter with other experiences. Hence where Simon claims that the mind performs an inventory activity akin to that of the machine's, he is grossly obviating the nature of the activity both agents perform respectively. The notion of an "inventory" is inapplicable for explaining what the mind does. For if one were to adopt Simon's inventory conception of recall it would mean that in recalling one actually "locates" spatial-temporal data in the brain and thereby "recalls." Yet what sense does it make to say that one "locates" an experience *in* the mind ? The locution of location loses its uniquely referential meaning when applied to acts of consciousness.

Attention must also be given to *how* one endeavors to respond to a command. The dominant factor here is the requirement that the action must be in the agent's external environment. For he must make a *judgment* that by doing such and such he will fulfil the command. Hence his deliberation is not simply the identification of an action as Simon suggests through his inventory conception of recollection, but rather the *estimation* that say this action *may* bring about the object understood by the command. An important point emerges here concerning the type of reasoning which animates the agent's action. For every external action by a human agent involves an inductive judgment. This covers even cases where apparently no deep reflection takes place, e.g. lifting a pencil. The justification of why one succeeds in lifting the pencil can only be traced back to the agent's belief that in the past similar behavior resulted in the desired effect. Hence he generalizes that in this case also an action like the one performed will work in the future. There is no deduction operative here as the reasoning behind the action.

The recognition of induction as the reasoning involved in responding to imperatives undercuts Simon's thesis in two ways. First, in order to fully understand what is involved in responses to imperatives one must account for the reasoning *within*, which initiates the action. This means that it is not enough to look at the human organism externally as a reactor to a complex outer environment. Here

Simon's thesis concerning the need for considering only the observable responses of the agent precipitates an incomplete view of such behavior, as far as its logic is concerned.

Secondly, all computers to date operate upon circuits exhibiting deductive functions. Thus any operation a computer performs : recording symbols, copying symbols, moving symbols, erasing symbols, and comparing symbols is the result of some deductive inference.[192] When it comes to imperatives, however, inductive reasoning is seen to be essential. It is in fact untenable to say that responses and commands can be handled within a deductive inference. For a command cannot be part of a deductive argument, since such arguments function only where premisses and conclusion are all indicatives. Thus by its nonindicatival nature a command can neither precede from nor precipitate to a deductive conclusion. It follows then that the deductive operations manifest in closed systems cannot extend to imperatives. Hence Simon's quickness in introducing the computer as an explanatory model falls under immediate suspicion.

Simon seeks to alleviate any difficulty resulting from the attempt to include commands into deductive operations by resurrecting J. Jörgensen's view that in every imperative there is an implied indicatival kernel, which serves as the basis for a logic of imperatives modeled upon propositional logic.[193] The derived indicative is said to "picture" the circumstances to be brought about should the imperative be acted upon.[194] Simon employs Jörgensen's view to show how mechanical decision making comes about. He thus describes the state referred to by the imperative's derived indicative as the *state* space. The problem in mechanical decision making is thus that of translating a specifiable *action* space, i.e. the range of actions which will successfully fulfil the command, into a specifiable state space. Simon also calls this the "design problem," since it involves relating actions to some desired end or state.[195] Though this type of problem *may* be associated with the heuristic issue of discovering the appropriate actions, it is distinct from the latter. For in the design problem the machine is faced with the *mapping* of actions onto possible states of the world, whereas heuristics concerns itself with finding and choosing these actions, while taking requirements of efficiency into account.[196]

Keeping within the framework of the organism as the simple reactor to a complex environment, Simon sees the design problem for humans as that of identifying *efferent* signals, which by altering the state of the environment, will produce the state conveyed to the organism through afferent signals (i.e. the conveyed command). Evidence as to the fact of this afferent-efferent alignment is found by Simon in the very use of natural language. He observes that there are many cases where verbs become nouned, e.g. "to wash." In this case the expression for the action of cleansing clothing serves to describe also the state of affairs of clothing having been cleaned—"the wash." Hence natural language in itself forms the web of interconnections between action language and state language. This supporting phenomenon, though not readily recognized in ordinary discourse, is said to result from the natural aim of all early learning, namely that of bringing about a state of affairs through an acquired knowledge of action.[197]

The difficulty Simon sought to remove through the intro-duction of Jörgensen's thesis remains. For the imperative still eludes a meaningful place within a deductive system. First, Simon unreflectingly trusts Jörgensen's rendition on how indicatives are derived from imperatives, and thus he is open to the same criticism Jörgensen is exposed to. What sense does it make to say that an imperative *implies* an indicatively expressed "picture" of the world, or that an indicative is *derivable* from some imperative ? Surely an imperative cannot be said to be true or false, and thus cannot imply anything in the intended sense of "logically implies". In an obscure way Jörgensen simply assumes that every imperative contains and thus implies an indica-tive, and that this is all one need to say. However, seeing the difficulty poised by the nonindicatival nature of imperatives reveals the shallowness of Jörgensen's assumption.

Secondly, Simon's entire presentation of mechanical designing is geared towards the articulation of a model for how humans respond to imperatives. However, Simon has not dealt with the imperative in his model. The "state space" he speaks of is an *indicatively* expressed "possible" state of affairs, concerning what it would be like *should* the imperative be correctly responded to. Again the "action space" refers to an *indicatively* expressed range of actions which will fulfil the command. Thus his rendition of the design problem is presented in terms of relating indicatives about actions with indicatives dealing with projected states of the world. Where is the role of the imperative in all of this ? Clearly, it has no involvement as a distinct grammatical entity in Simon's account of design. Moreover, it cannot be claimed that the "state space" compensates for what is expressed by an imperative, since an imperative requires action, whereas the "state space" describes the *results* of actions. Neither can the "action space" serve as a vehicle for expressing what an imperative conveys, since an imperative need not specify the kind of action which is to be employed. The "action space," however, must indicate a range of successful actions.

Thus in the presentation of the activity of designing, the imperative is not involved. The mechanical design model thus does not catch the function of the imperative as understood in natural language. Consequently, the original issue of how imperatives are going to be handled within a deductive system remains unanswered.

Of equal interest is his point concerning how ordinary language mirrors within itself mechanical design activity. For Simon was seen to hold that nouned verbs result from the mind's inclination to connect the action expressed by a verb, say "to wash," with the result of that action, the nouned verb "the wash."

What is not clear is how the nouning of verbs supports Simon's assumed correspondence between mechanical design-

ing and intentional human responses. Is it the very nouning of
verbs which indicates that the above correspondence exists?
Why ? Simon tries to hint at an answer by saying that the
case in point results from the way learning itself inclines
towards connecting acquired actions with desired states of
the world.   However, why cannot the nouning of verbs be
explained by alluding to the subject-predicate morphology
of sentences, which necessitates the substantivizing of whatever is presented as the predicate of a sentence.   Furthermore, the use of the expression "the wash" can be traced
to some arbitrary convention, for which the expression
"that pile of cloths" can be used in a suitable context.
Hence there is nothing in the expression "the wash" to
suggest that there is a *necessary* connotation of transforming an action state into a state of the world.   "The wash"
can simply be the name of an object.

Thus far the investigation of Simon's thesis has dealt
with his "linguistic argument" and how it is supposed to
support the claimed parallelism between mechanical movements and intentional human responses. However, Simon
is seen to have no argument here. For once he decides
upon presenting the human organism as a simple reactor
to a complex outer environment, he distorts the human
element he is confronted with. The latter is the natural
language operative in everyday communication, containing
imperatives as independent grammatically functional elements. What occurs then throughout the writings cited is
an effort to construe mechanistically every term pertaining
to human responses to commands. Thus where he speaks of
the mind's inventory process, its attending to pertinent
areas of experience, its mapping of actions onto states of
the world, the verb-noun relation in ordinary language, etc.
he is already dealing with a mechanical idea of intentional
behavior. Yet he desires to pass on this view of human
behavior as the more veracious. As a result, since at the
outset he has reduced man to a machine, the parallelism he
seeks to establish is nonexistent.

Simon introduces a second ("heuristic") argument to

further underscore the view that a calculus of imperatives can be expressed through propositional logic by focusing upon the particular way a machine arrives at a unique response. Assuming that the human organism functions like a computer, he argues that the case where a mechanical response exhibits heuristic activity can be made to explain the human reasoning involved in imperatival communication. For the human agent also tests different courses of action so as to come up with a successful mode of behavior in *nontrivial* situations. This human searching activity is expressable in terms of a machanical heuristic programme, that is, as any variant of the General Problem Solver (G.P.S.) found in computers.[198]

Specifically, a machine solves for a mathematical theorem, conceived as an ordered series of syntactically well-formed sentences and symbolized by 'T' (for terminal state), by finding the sequence of operators which will transform some initial state containing axioms, previously proved theorems, and mathematical rules of inference, and symbolized by 'A', into T. Depending upon whether the machine is operating upon optimal or sufficient effeciency, it proceeds to compare the state designated by 'A' and that designate by 'T'. By determining the differences between them, and by means of a table of connections, G.P.S. applies logical operators to each of these differences and thus transforms A into T.[199]

Relative to the human agent, Simon sees the logic of action in human responses reflecting the above mechanical heuristic rationale. For example, he observes that the human agent must deal with the following conditional when faced with any command (i.e. any terminal state T) say "Try to achieve T" : "..., if at time t_0 the world is not in state T, then it can sometimes be brought into that state at t, by performing the planning action, P(T), followed by the performance section D [P(T)], ..." Assuming that this conditional is *discovered* to be true (i.e. state A) the command then *really* expresses the following true statement : "The state of the world at t_1 *is* (my italics) T." For if the agent

performs the planning action P with regard to T, and this
is followed through with the performance action D upon P,
then the state of the world at t_1 *must* be T. Hence what
one has here is the conversion of a state A into a state T by
the agent's appropriate action.[200]

Simon recognizes that in "real life" there is often little
guarantee that a novel course of action will yield the
desired end. For this reason he analyses the command
with the introductory : "try to." The latter allows for the
flexibility needed to give expression to situations where
the planning or performing actions are new and untried.
He goes on to state the varied meaning of "Try to achieve
T." as "...(1) to execute the programme P(T); (2) if (P) has
no output, stop; (3) if P(T) has the output P', execute the
programme D(P')."[201] Thus the formal implications of the
imperative for Simon are dependent on the success of the
agent hitting upon a successful mode of responding. The
responsive success of the agent then becomes the way of
determining the actual *meaning* of the imperative.

Simon characterizes the rational process in which imperatives are responded to as the relationship between states,
the initial state encompassing the actions the agent
discovers, and the terminal state referring to the condition
to be brought about. Yet the dominant question is to
what "state" does a command in ordinary discourse refer.
There is surely a functional difference between a command
prescribing a state of affairs to come about, and a statement
referring to that state of affairs. In prescribing something,
the final object is not referred to, since no single terminal
entity as yet exists to which there can be a reference. Hence,
what does Simon mean where he says that an imperative in
ordinary discourse can be taken as referring to a "terminal
state ?" Surely it cannot be claimed that a prescriptive
both refers to a definite state of the world, and also prescribes that this same state of the world come about. Yet it
is this contradictory referring and prescribing function of
imperatives which Simon's mechanistic conception of
human heuristic rationale entails and also makes it
untenable.

The divergence between the computer and the human organism is thus due to the simple fact that machines are *not* given commands. For *any* "instructions" given to a computer are composed of the following elements : *initialization* (i.e. an explicit specification of the function to be evaluated), *calculation* (i.e. an explicit specification of a point at which to begin), *substitution* (i.e. an explicit specification of how to go on from the starting point), *testing* (i.e. an explicit specification that the computer list a number of answers, and *completion* (i.e. an explicit specification of when the problem will be solved).[202] All of these components must be involved in telling a machine what to do. However, a command given to a human agent does not essentially contain the above factors. For example, if someone is being tested, the command given him would not delineate what to look for, where to begin, how to continue looking, how many possible responses are required, and when to stop. A command in ordinary discourse simply prescribes the bringing about of a state of affairs by telling the agent to *bring it about*. Apart from assuming a common language between imperator and agent, the agent is not *primed* to react in the way a machine must be in order for it to retrieve information. For this reason one speaks of the commands given to humans as genuine prescriptives, whereas the instructions given to computers are indicatives which *refer* to specific operations already within the machine. When a computer is fed these indicatives (i.e. instructions) they set up a "passage" of activity through which the computer proceeds to bring forth the data already stored within it.[203]

Moreover, the fact that imperatives in themselves cannot refer to the state of affairs they prescribe contradicts his intent in interpreting imperatives with the "try to" locution. It is recalled that Simon seeks to reinterpret the imperative as conveyed in ordinary discourse by means of "try to" so as to make allowance for the contingency where a course of action does not successfully fulfil the command. However, if he is going to apply the mechanical model to the human organism, then the imperative must *refer* to the terminal state spoken of in the imperative, in which case it makes no sense to say "*try to* achieve that state."

On the other hand, Simon also encounters difficulties where he assumes that the human organism contains within itself an "initial state" similar to that of a computer's. For whatever is said to constitute the initial state, e.g. previous actions, etc., it can never be a state in humans wherein its contents are absolutely certain. Surely the contingency inherent in the expectation that a past course of action will yield the desired result severely limits one's saying that the initial state found in machines is identifiable also in the human rationale. For it makes no sense to say that a machine "doubts" its initial states, i.e. the courses of action which have been programmed into it. Yet it is meaningful to say of a human being that he doubts the effectiveness of the course of action he is familiar with in a new situation. Thus again there is a defect in the procedure which seeks to employ the computer to explain human heuristic activity. In this case, because of the element of contingent effectiveness in all human action, the "initial state" of machines has no counterpart in a description of human responses.

The absence of this "initial state" in a description of human heuristic rationale also calls attention to the dominant *modal* element inherent in responding to a command. In part Simon seeks to accommodate the element of possibility which is present in any response to a command by noting that there is a conditional involved in all attempts at responding to commands. Where this conditional turns out to be true, then the conveyed imperative is said to express a true indicative. However, this recognition of a conditional as in a way animating the action which leads to the fulfilment of an imperative is a concession to the view that the modal element is a prominent and unavoidable factor in any attempt to articulate a logic of imperatives. Hence one has here the further undermining of Simon's general position that imperatival discourse can be shown to involve *only* indicatives, and thus modal logic is not needed for articulating a logic of imperatives.

Hence Simon's "heuristic argument" for the view that a logic of commands can be modelled upon a computer's programmed movements fails since it assumes that (1) imperatives in ordinary discourse both prescribe and refer to the same state of affairs, and (2) the initial states manifest in computers are present also in human agents. These unfounded assumptions prevent Simon from securing his ultimate claim that the two valued propositional logic underlying the operations of computers can be used to present a logic of imperatives and responses to them. Consequently, Simon must either accept the need for some sort of modal logic in presenting his logic of imperatives, or re-analyse imperatives so as to somehow fit them into two valued logic.

The intriguing issue Simon raises through his effort at evolving a logic of imperatives is not whether machines think, but rather whether humans think like machines. In support of the latter he seeks to reduce man to a machine by characterizing human behavior in terms which are applicable only for computers, and by conceiving human heuristic rationale in terms of mechanical heuristics. The shortcomings of his efforts result from the evident failure to realize that the language intended for the description of precise mechanical behavior is inapplicable in the description of human behavior, and that factors essential to mechanical heuristics (e.g. initial and terminal states) are not manifest in human reflection. Consequently, Simon's allusion to mechanical models so as to present a two valued logic of imperatives is not acceptable.

PART II

"SOME STEPS FORWARD"

7

The Pragmatic Structure of Imperative Discourse

Apart from the contextualist analyses surveyed above, there appears to be an awakening realization that the logic of imperatives should be purused from an extensional rather than an intensional mode of analysis. This at least seems to be the view of G.B. Keene, who in "Can Commands Have Logical Consequences?" argues that Williams makes a too sweeping claim in denying the possibility of imperative inference. While supporting Rescher against Williams in this respect, Keene briefly says at the end of his article that one should not look for a *logical entailment* between uttered commands, but rather one should consider a *pragmatic relation* between uttered commands, which is "parallel" to the entailment relation holding between asserted statements. Keene also grants that such a pragmatic relation has as yet been unexplored, but it seems to require some notion of an *inclusion* between various kinds of actions.[204]

Though Keene's remarks are highly tentative, they do provide a means whereby one can proceed to offer an extensional and pragmatic logic of imperatives. For what has been said thus far on the logic of imperatives, apart from Mrs. Beardsley's contributions, seems to be plagued with the issue of how such a logic is at all possible. Keene's view at least indicates a new procedure, which can be pursued without dealing with the problems that plague the intensionalists. At least this is the perspective within which the comments that follow are presented.

The aim of the present chapter is to develop some pertinent points concerning the study of semiotics, and then to proceed with an extensional and pragmatic analysis of imperatives as sentences. Though this approach is different from that undertaken by the intensionalists, its relation to the latter will be discussed in the subsequent and final chapter. Here the sole aim is the pragmatic analysis of sentences which express relations extensionally involved by imperatives, and also those relations involved in direct responses to imperatives.

It is important to stress as well that the above investigation should be viewed in the context of the developments which have taken place in the history of this issue. For as the review of the literature clearly shows, the intensionalists have never satisfactorily answered the question of how imperatives are to be handled in a two-valued propositional logic. Moreover, because of their failure in this respect, their logic have suffered from the very weakness of their foundations. Indeed, most recently it has been seen that intensionalists have sought to counter the ominous position of B.A.O. Williams, who denies that a logic of imperatives is even possible along the line thus far suggested. Thus as a means of defending the general view that a logic of imperatives is feasible, the following extensional and pragmatic analysis is offered. Basically it is hoped that by using this approach more ground can be cleared as to what is involved in giving and acting upon imperatives. For one of the problems which permeates the attempts reviewed thus far is a failure by most writers to agree upon even the most elemental aspects of imperatives and imperative discourse.

Ultimately, the following analysis will be aimed at developing a logic of imperatives. In this respect the extensional and pragmatic approach will be tested, insofar as it can cope with the issues which bedevil the intensionalists. However, it must be pointed out that because of the differences in the intensionalist and extensionalist approaches, many of the problems which are peculiar to the former are foreign to the latter. However, just how this comes about is the theme of the subsequent chapter.

Section 1. *Syntactics, Semantics, and Pragmatics*

Generally, the study of signs, or *semiotics*, is divided into three cumulative levels : syntactics, semantics, and pragmatics. In the first level one studies the relations between or among signs. More precisely, syntactics deals with how signs concatenate to form expressions. From this simpler description of syntactics one sees how the levels mentioned are closely interconnected. For in considering what constitutes a finite concatenation of signs one is treading into the area of what constitutes a *meaningful* (complete) expression, which is part of the province of semantics. Within semantics there are two domains : the *theory of meaning* and the *theory of reference*. In the former area one finds problems dealing with synonymy, significance and analyticity. In the latter domain are the issues concerning naming, truth, denotation, and extension.[205] Here again the interconnection of the levels of semiotics becomes manifest. For in attempting to determine the significance of a term, or its denotation, one must in some way face the issue of how the said term is used by the person who employs it. Thus one enters into the domain of pragmatics, where one deals with the relation of the user of a language and that language itself.

That aspect of semantics which will underlie the analysis which follows is the denotative or *designative* aspect. Thus without entering into the discussion of imperatives it is important to define as carefully as possible the sense in which "denotation" will be understood. With some refinements the definition of C.I. Lewis in "The Modes of Meaning" appears sufficient. Lewis states that the "*denotation* of a term is the class of all actual or existent things to which the term correctly applies." Here "denotation" is taken as interchangeable with "designation."[206]

He elucidates this definition by noting that the phrase "actual or existent" is meant to be limiting in the sense that those things that would be or are namable by the term, but which cannot in fact exist, are not included within the denotation of the term. Thus also it is seen that in his definition the phrase "correctly applies" really means the correct *naming* by the term of the actual or existent thing.[207]

The notion of "denotation" is not altered when viewed from the pragmatic level of analysis. For in considering the denotation of a term when it is used by someone, *the denotation* of the term itself is not in any way changed. Furthermore, the denoting by a term may be of interest on the pragmatic level, as well as the fact that one is "using" the said term. For example, the word 'apple' designates all actual or existent things called (or named) 'apples.' In so considering the word one is reflecting upon its function in denoting apples. This function is termed the "use" of the word "apple." On the other hand, in considering the word 'apple' as it is used by someone to designate apples, one is reflecting upon the word's denotation *as well as* the fact that someone is using the word 'apples' to denote apples in some special cases.

In order to avoid areas of vagueness, the extensional and pragmatic approach will be employed only in cases where it can reveal something about the ostensibly determinable relations of individuals using language. In this way the analysis which follows does not deal with the user's personal reflection upon the language he employs.

Also, unlike the purely semantic level of analysis where one may be concerned only with the denotatum of a particular word or expression, the extensional and pragmatic investigation of terms which denote involves considering the structure of sentences, which have the user of the language as subject and a word's or expression's denotatum as their predicate, connected by an empirically determinable pragmatic relation. For example, the extensional and pragmatic analysis of the case where John recites his lesson is expressed as follows :   (i) 'J Rec^t L'.

Thus where 'J' stands for John, 'Rec' stands for the relational action of reciting, 't' stands for the time during which John recites, and 'L' stands for a lesson, formula (i) illustrates the structure of a sentence expressing John's reciting his lesson at time t.

Thus in the discussion which follows, an attempt will be made to determine the structure of sentences expressing the ostensibly determinable relations involved in the giving and responding to imperatives. By this means it is hoped that a complete extensional and pragmatic characterization of the discourse involving imperatives can be achieved.

It may be asked, however, what sort of relations are expressed by formulas such as (i), and why they should be any more coveted than relations determined through intensional analyses of language. In the first place it is proposed that the relations which will be set forth in the forthcoming analysis are *ideal* relations, in the sense that they are relations which are always involved when an individual uses language to effect some end. Thus also, they are relations which are manifest in whatever language one uses, as long as his use of that language is rational. In essence they are relations about an individual's *behavior* when using natural language.

It remains to be explained, however, why such relations are more illustrative than relations resulting from intensional analysis of language. Here it is important to repeat the aim of the proposed study from the point of view of what has come before. For it was seen that the intensional analyses of imperatives involved highly complex conceptions of imperatives, which are more often than not obscure as to what is meant by an imperative so conceived. Hence it is hoped that by concentrating upon the objectively determinable denotatum of imperatives, and upon how ostensibly determinable behavior is involved in giving and responding upon imperative, as sharper and more plausible conception of imperatival discourse can be arrived at. For these reasons the extensional and pragmatic analysis of imperatives is pursued.

Section 2. *The Structure of Imperative Dicsourse*

Elementary to the study of the extension of discourse involving imperatives is the analysis of the extension of imperatives generally. Here it can be said that on the whole all imperatives refer to physical action or action to be performed by an agent upon some object at a particular time, so as to effect some desired property on that object. Using appropriate symbolism one can write that imperative sentence I_s refers to a physical action f to be performed on an object z with means y at time t to effect property F. In short 'I_s' is to stand for 'fxyFt', which is to be considered as an expression for the extension of 'I_s'.

Accordingly, the presentation of the extensional pragmatics of commands will be developed along the lines suggested by Wittgenstein in the *Philosophical Investigations*. There commands are seen in terms of their performative manifestation. This is to say that for Wittgenstein, understanding that one has obeyed a command requires the examination of some performance in light of criteria. Thus commands themselves are essentially linguistic means of illiciting actions from some agent, and this is all that the analysis of their meaning can involve. For this reason the presentation of the extension of any command above is rendered in such a way so as to emphasize the elements involved in the agent's expected performance.[208]

The next question dealing with discourse involving imperatives is what constitutes the "conveying" of an imperative. The solution here rests on how the extensional and pragmatic viewpoint is conceived, and upon the actual relations found to make up the giving of an imperative. Thus, recalling that this analysis involves *ostensibly determinable* cases involving language and its users, the determination of how such cases are involved in the giving of imperatives becomes a major concern.

Since the conveying of an imperative is taken as involving only the ostensibly determinable, one must make sure that no subjective connotations are involved in the locution which relates the imperator to that which he gives as an imperative. However, it is difficult to find in English a term which is sufficiently free of intimations that a mental disposition is implied by such a word. This is specifically true of such words as "asserting," "demanding," "intending," "imperatizing," etc. For this reason it is best to refer to the Greek notion of "*diataso*" to define the pragmatic relation of an imperator "commanding" an imperative. For "*diataso*" means "to set, arrange, to set in order, ..., to appoint to do or be..."[209] Thus the word "*diataso*" conveys the idea of an imperator's empirically determinable performing or arranging and/or setting in order that something be brought about by some agent. Furthermore, "*diataso*" also means the communicating or uttering to someone that something be done. Thus by this one notion, which will be translated as "commanding," one is able to express the event of someone arranging that something be brough about, and his communicating to someone that such and such is to be done.

Hence the primitive 'Com' will be used to stand for the act of arranging for the bringing about of some end *and* for the imperator's uttering of an imperative to effect his end. Therefore, where 'M' stands for an imperator, 'A' stands for an agent, 'x' stands for some physical object, 'f' stands for the action upon the object, 'y' stands for a means of acting, 'F' stands for some property of x, 't' stands for the time at which the imperator commands, and 't_c' stands for the time at which the imperative is intended to be fulfilled, the structure of a sentence expressing the giving of an imperative may be set down as:

(1)   'M Com^t A, 'f x y F t_c".

Formula (1) expresses the relation that M commands at time t that 'agent A perform action f on object x with means y to effect property F at time t_c. 'Thus formula (1) may serve as expressing the structure of the sentence saying that someone commands someone else e.g. to throw a switch. Here 'M' will denote the imperator, 'A' will denote the agent who is to do the throwing, 'x' would name the switch to be thrown, 'f' would be the agent's action of throwing, 'y' would name the means of action, 'F' would name the property of being a thrown switch, 't' would name the time at which M commands A, and 't_c' would be the time at which M wants A to throw the switch. In most cases, however, reference to "means" need not be stated in the command.

The strangeness of the pragmatic relation expressed by 'Com' lies in the fact that in English one speaks of the act of uttering an imperative apart from the act of intending by a command that an end come about. However, if one were to consider the imperator's uttering separately from his intention, major difficulties arise. For if M's uttering is said to occur only after M has explained his intention, then his intention must be expressed as prior to his act of uttering imperative sentence I_s. Hence one gets into the formidable problem of how one can express in an extensional manner the "nonobservable" case of M's personally intending that his imperative bring about such and such. On the other hand, if M's uttering of I_s is regarded without M's intention, then one is faced with the difficulty of handling an "intentionless" imperative utterance. For these reasons a view which *simultaneously* includes both M's ostensibly determinable arranging for some end, *and* his uttering of an imperative sentence, seems advantageous.

Though (1) expresses the case of giving an imperative, the question of what constitutes the communication of or the conveying of an imperative has not been fully answered. For one must go on to give the analysis of the case where an agent carries out the imperator's command. It makes little sense to present the case of M commanding I_s to A, without also showing through the same type of analysis that there is an agent who may or may not accept I_s.

Thus what is required here is the expression of the way agent A responds to the imperator's command. Staying within the conditions of an extensional analysis one must look upon the case of the agent's acceptance or non-acceptance of the imperative I_s as the case where the agent either acts or does not act upon the imperative. A new primitive is introduced to express the agent's action. Thus 'Acpt' expresses the acting upon the commanded imperative by A. This primitive does not express anything about the 'success' of the agent's action in fulfilling M's imperative. 'Acpt' only refers to the agent acting upon receiving the imperative. Also, this primitive of itself says nothing about A's personal understanding of the imperative. For the conditions of A's understanding the imperator's utterance is assumed by this analysis, along with the assumptions that M and A are both rational human beings, who speak the same language, and who are within conversational proximity to each other.

The structure of sentences dealing with A's acceptance of M's commanded imperative may be set down as follows:

(2)   'A Acpt $^{t1+}$ 'fxyFt$_c$', Com M, t'.

The above formula expresses the structure of a sentence about an agent who accepts at time t_{1+} to 'effect action f on object x with means y to bring about property F at the required time t_c,' as commanded by M, at time t. In passing it is to be noted that a time sequence now exists between the relation expressed by (1) and that expressed by (2). For the agent cannot be said to accept I_s prior to its being commanded.

In contrast to the notion of "acceptance" presented above there is that of "nonacceptance" or "rejection". As in the case of "acceptance," there is no intimation about the agent's success or failure in fulfilling M's imperative where the notion of "nonacceptance" is used. It only expressed the idea that the agent does not elect to act upon the command which is directed to him. Thus using the primitive '—Acpt' to express the pragmatic notion of an agent ignoring a command, the following relation results :

(3)   'A—Acpt $^{t1+}$ 'fxyF t$_c$,'Com M,t'.

Formula (3) illustrates the structure of a sentence dealing with the agent A not accepting at time t_{1+} to 'effect
action f on object x with means y to bring about property
F at the required time t_c, as commanded by M at time t.'
It is to be noted that because both relations expressed by
(2) and (3) occur within the same time-span t to t_{1+}, and
since both relations are contrary to each other, one cannot
say that (2) and (3) express relations which occur simultaneously.

Thus considering an imperative commanded in the sense
of *diataso*, and an agent who accepts or does not accept the
commanded imperative, then the said imperative is conceived of as "conveyed." Thus the "conveying" of an imperative may now be presented as either the conjunction of the
imperator's commanding an imperative and an agent's
acceptance of it, or the conjunction of the imperator's
commanding an imperative and the agent's non-acceptance
of it. Using the symbol 'Con' to express the relation of
"conveying," the latter notion may be symbolically expressed as :

(T1) ($(Com^t A,$ 'fxyFt_c'). (A Acpt $^{t1+}$ 'fxyFt_c', Com M,t))$\equiv$
       (M Con^{t1+}A, I_s).

Theorem (T1) states that the conjunction of imperator
M commanding A to do I_s at t *and* the agent's acceptance
of I_s as commanded by M is equivalent to M having *conveyed* to A I_s at time t_{1+}.

The above theorem expresses the extensional and pragmatic relation of conveying an imperative. However, unlike the notions of "commanding" or "accepting" in themselves, the idea of "conveying" an imperative is complex,
since it involves the activity of both an imperator and an
agent. Yet the notion of "conveying" nonethless is extensional and pragmatic since it is given in terms of such extensional and pragmatic relations, that is "commanding"
and "accepting."

Another way of presenting the notion of "conveying" an
imperative is as follows :

(T2) $((M \ Com^{t_1} \ A \ \text{'fxyFt}_c\text{'}). \ (A—Acpt \ ^{t_1+}\text{"fxy Ft}_c\text{'}, ComM,t))$
$\equiv (M \ Con^{t_1+}A,I_s).$

_ Theorem (T2) states that the conjunction of M commanding I_s to A at t *and* the agent's refusal to act upon I_s at t^{1+} as commanded by M is equivalent to M conveying I_s to A at time t^{1+}.

Here it may be objected that one cannot express the conveying of an imperative both as the acceptance to act upon a commanded imperative, and also as the agent's refusal to act upon the imperative as commanded by M. However, such an objection assumes that to act upon an imperative is an action, where refusal to act upon an imperative is not an action. This assumption is false, since the relation designated by '—Acpt' is just as much an ostensibly determinable activity as that of acting upon an imperative. For one's refusal to act upon an imperative by ignoring it because it violates his moral standards, phyical abilities, etc., constitutes an activity. The fact that one understands the command, and justifies his not fulfilling it by stating that it violates some personal belief, illustrates that the intended agent is doing something, though it is not that of acting upon an imperative. Hence in theorems (T1) and (T2) one is presenting the notion of "conveying" an imperative in terms of two different kinds of actions relating to reacting to the imperative.

From (T1) and (T2) it is seen that an imperative is not conveyed if M does not command. Thus where an individual says that his actions result from acting upon an imperative, but where in fact no imperative was given to him, then an imperative had not been conveyed, and the agent's actions are somehow erroneous. Also, if someone gives a command in the sense of *diataso*, but there is no agent to whom it is addressed, and who can act upon the imperative, then again the said imperative cannot be conveyed. The latter would be the case where M gives an imperative, but no one hears it.

Finally, the time at which an imperative is said to be conveyed, t_{1+}, should be looked upon as the time-span beginning at t, where M commands the imperative, and ending at time t_1 , when M accepts the imperative. This time-span may have an indefinite number of periods (smaller time-spans than t to t_{1+}) at which the agent either accepts or does not accept the commanded imperative. Thus the time-span t to t_{1+} covers "part of" the time-span during which the agent and the imperator discourse imperativally. The rest of the time-span covering all the duration of imperatival discourse involves the time at which the agent "performs" the requirements of the imperative. However, the notion of the agent's "performance" will be discussed shortly.

An important step resulting from the analysis of what is involved in "conveying" an imperative is that now one is able to state how commands are "genuine" or "nongenuine." However, it is best to state clearly what is meant by a nongenuine command. Certainly it is not claimed that an imperative by itself, e.g. "Shut the door !", is nongenuine because in the context in which it is given there is no door to be closed. Such a conception of a nongenuine imperative leads one into saying that the imperative in question *states* or assumes something to be the case which is factually false. However, what is meant by saying that an imperative *states* something which is false ? Imperatives, by themselves, do not *state* anything factual. Their sole use is to *order* some thing to come about. They are not vehicles by which to state or imply facts. The statement of facts is something one does by means of indicatives.

However, the sense in which an imperative would be held to be nongenuine in this discussion is that of the imperator erroneously commanding (ordering or arranging) that something is to be done. Here it is seen that the emphasis is placed upon the error in the imperator's commanding that such and such be brought about, and not upon the imperative he gives. Thus it is the imperative as considered in an extensional and pragmatic sense, as 'imperator-commanding-the imperative sentence,' which is said to be genuine or nongenuine.

Having stated the above, it may now be asked when a command is genuine or nongenuine. Here it is claimed that a command in the sense indicated is said to be genuine or nongenuine if it implies conditions which are logically, physically, and/or technically possible or impossible. For example, to command "Draw a round square !" is to command something which implies the logically impossible. Thus this is a case of nongenuine commanding. It is a case where the imperator is not "properly" commanding, that is arranging to bring about, that something come about, since he is assuming the logically impossible : drawing a round square. It is important to stress again that it is the *commanding* which is termed "nongenuine," and not just the command. More precisely, given that the relation of commanding is a formalized relation between imperator, agent, and imperative sentence, the case of "nongenuine commanding" would be that of incorrectly instantiating into the formalized relation of commanding. For where one commands someone to do something logically impossible, then he is not considering the agent as an agent when he is addressing him (since the agent can never draw a round square), and the so-called imperative the imperator gives does not function as an imperative (since it cannot bring anything about). Thus in such cases there is no relation of commanding taking place, and anyone employing formula (1) to illustrate what happens in this case is incorrectly instantiating into formula (1).

Furthermore, commanding may be nongenuine where the imperator assumes something which is physically or technically impossible. Thus one has a nongenuine command where the imperator says : "Lift the Empire State Building with one finger !" The commanding here is nongenuine because it involves doing something which is physically impossible for any man to do. Also the command : "Make me a Stradivarious violin !" is nongenuine, since the secret of how such violins are made is now lost, and barring its rediscovery, such an imperative is technically impossible to fulfil.

The nongenuine imperative should be distinguished from the meaningless imperative. An imperative such as "Sing me a bar of exuberant soap!" does not convey any meaningful directive to the agent. Though this command may have the form of an imperative in so far as it is introduced by a phrase like "sing me" and is ended by an exclamation mark, it does not convey any meaningful command to the agent, as the phrase "sing me a bar of soap" illustrates. On the other hand, a nongenuine imperative is meaningful in the sense that it requires that something intelligible is to be done, but that which is to be done is for some reason impossible.

The conveying of an imperative was found to be complex in so far as it involves both the imperator's act of arranging that something come about and the agent's act of responding to the imperator's command that something be brought about. Similarly, the case of *fulfilling* an imperative, from the point of view of the extensional and pragmatic analysis also involves actions by *both* agent and imperator. Just how this comes about is the next topic of concern.

Granting that an agent accepts an imperative, in the sense that he acts upon it, one must next consider the case of the agent fulfilling I_s within the time-span t to t_c. What is involved in this latter case is the "performance" of the imperative sentence. However, the acts of performing are distinguished from A's acceptance of I_s. For A's acceptance is taken only in the very wide sense of the agent's response, however, deals with a number of acts intended by A to satisfy the imperative. Though the events of the agent's performing may be held as reacting to I_s, they differ from acceptance in that they constitute to *complete* reaction of A to I_s.

The pragmatics of performance has been discussed by Professor Richard M. Martin, and it is largely his views which are adopted here to explain the relation between the agent and what he is seen to perform.[210]

The primitive employed to express the pragmatic relation of agent A to what he performs is 'Prfm'. Thus the struc-

ture of sentences dealing with event of A's performance may
be rendered as :

(4)   'A Prfm$^{t1+\ to\ tc}$f,x,y,F,t$_c$'.

The above formula illustrates the structure of a sentence
about A performing during time-span t$_1$ to t$_c$ action f on
object x with means y to effect property F at the required
time t$_c$.[211]

It is observed that by means of (4) one can express a
number of events occurring at different moments in the time-
span t$_1$ to t$_c$, which are the occurrences of A's acts in his
progress towards satisfying I$_s$. It would be equally correct
if instead of (4) a series of formulas were given to express
different performances by A during the moments of time-
span of t$_1$ to t$_c$. For economy, however, (4) is employed to
cover all actions performed by A to satisfy the imperative.

By itself the performance of the agent does not constitute
the event of satisfying the imperative I$_s$. For the imperator,
or any observer, must survey the agent's performance, to
determine whether aspects of its designation are identical to
the designation of what is required by M's imperative.

Thus where the various designata making up the directive of a commanded imperative (that is making up 'fxyFt$_c$')
are *identical* to the designata of the various aspects making
up the agent's performance, then it may be said in an extensional and pragmatic sense that the agent has "successfully
performed" the commanded imperative. Introducing the
symbol '*Prfm*' to express the notion of "successful performance," the following theorem may be set down :

(T3)   ((M Con^{t1+}A, I$_s$). (A Prfm$^{t1+totc}$f, x, y, F, t$_c$))$\equiv$

           (A *Prfm*^{tc}'fxyFt$_c$', Com M, t).

Theorem (T3) states that where imperator M conveys at time
t$_{1+}$ to agent A imperative sentence I$_s$ *and* agent A performs
during time-span t$_{1+}$ to t$_c$ action f, on object x, wiih means y,
to effect property F, at time t$_c$, is equivalent to A successfully performing at time t$_c$ the imperative 'fxyFt$_c$' as it is
commanded by M at t. (T3) holds only if the designata of

the different aspects of the agent's performance are identical to that of the performance required by the "conveyed" (Con) imperative.

In light of Theorem (T3) one is able to distinguish between the notion of the "successful performance" of imperative and the more general notion of "performance" referred to by 'Prfm'. In the case of the latter one is considering the relation between someone performing an action, upon some object, with some means, etc. However, in the case of "successfully performing an imperative" the notion of performance is restricted to the action upon an imperative directed to the agent. Thus the idea conveyed by *Prfm* is more limited than that expressed by Prfm.

In view of what has been said about the successful performing of imperatives, it can now be claimed that an acceptable direct response to an imperative is a true sentence stating that the agent performs the commanded imperative. Thus Theorem (T3) may be taken as expressing the structure of a sentence, which is a direct response to an imperative.

Of equal interest is the way in which one can say that an imperative is not successfully performed by an agent. For by observing the different aspects in which the imperator surveys the agent's performance, that is, with respect to the action f, object acted upon x, means of action y, resulting property F, and time of performing t_c, one finds a variety of ways in agent is said not to successfully perform I_s. The best means of illustrating this diverse means of not successfully performing I_s is by the following tables, which illustrate the various ways in which the designata of the performance required by the commanded imperative is not identical to the designata of the agent's performance.[212]

1.	2.	3.	4.	5.
$f_1 \neq f_2$	$f_1 \neq f_2$	$f_1 \neq f_2$	$f_1 \neq f_2$	$f_1 \neq f_2$
$x_1 = x_2$	$x_1 \neq x_2$	$x_1 \neq x_2$	$x_1 \neq x_2$	$x_1 \neq x_2$
$y_1 = y_2$	$y_1 = y_2$	$y_1 \neq y_2$	$y_1 \neq y_2$	$y_1 \neq y_2$
$F_1 = F_2$	$F_1 = F_2$	$F_1 = F_2$	$F_1 \neq F_2$	$F_1 \neq F_2$
$t_{c1} = t_{c2}$	$t_{c1} = t_{c2}$	$t_{c1} = t_{c2}$	$t_{c1} = t_{c2}$	$t_{c1} \neq t_{c2}$

6.	7.	8.	9.	10.
$f_1 = f_2$	$f_1 = f_2$	$f_1 = f_2$	$f_1 = f_2$	$f_1 = f_2$
$x_1 = x_2$	$x_1 = x_2$	$x_1 = x_2$	$x_1 \neq x_2$	$x_1 = x_2$
$y_1 = y_2$	$y_1 = y_2$	$y_1 \neq y_2$	$y_1 \neq y_2$	$y_1 \neq y_2$
$F_1 = F_2$	$F_1 \neq F_2$	$F_1 \neq F_2$	$F_1 \neq F_2$	$F_1 \neq F_2$
$t_{c1} \neq t_2$	$t_{c1} \neq t_{c2}$	$t_{c1} \neq t_{c2}$	$t_{c1} \neq t_{c2}$	$t_{c1} = t_{c2}$

11.	12.	13.
$f_1 \neq f_2$	$f_1 = f_2$	$f_1 = f_2$
$x_1 = x_2$	$x_1 \neq x_2$	$x_1 \neq x_2$
$y_1 = y_2$	$y_1 \neq y_2$	$y_1 \neq y_2$
$F_1 = F_2$	$F_1 \neq F_2$	$F_1 \neq F_2$
$t_{c1} \neq t_{c2}$	$t_{c1} = t_{c2}$	$t_{c1} = t_{c2}$

In 1. there is illustrated the case where the agent performs the wrong action on the appropriate object, with the correct means, and effects the right property at the desired time.

In 2. there is the case where the agent performs the wrong action on the wrong object, but acts with the proper means, and effects the desired property, at the appointed time.

3. illustrates the case where the agent does the wrong action, on the wrong object, with the wrong means, but effects the desired property at the appointed time.

In case 4. the agent employs the wrong action, on the wrong object, with the wrong means, and effects the wrong property at the appointed time.

In 5. every aspect of the agent's performance is wrong.

In case 6. there is illustrated the event where the agent is early or late in managing the imperative.

In 7. one has the agent performing the proper action, on the proper object, with the proper means, but he ends up with the wrong property at a time other than the one specified.

In 8. the agent employs the proper action on the proper object, but uses the wrong means and gets the wrong property, at the time which he is to bring about the imperative.

Case 9. illustrates the case where all that is correct with the agent's performance is that he performs the requested action.

Again, in 10. one has the case where the agent performs the appropriate action on the proper object, but he employs the wrong means, and effects the wrong property at the time desired.

Furthermore, in case 11. one has the situation where the agent employs a wrong action on the appropriate object with the correct means and produces the required effect at the wrong time.

In case 12. one has the agent reacting with the correct action on the wrong object with the means and effects the required property at the appropriate time.

Finally, in the last case 13. one has the agent employing the correct action on the wrong object with the wrong means, which results in the wrong property occurring at the appropriate time.

All cases from 1. through 13. are possibilities in which the agent does not fulfil the imperative commanded by M. Presumedly, if the notion of "performance" were expanded to include many more facets, then more cases of the agent mismanaging the imperator's command can be shown. Also; it is to be observed that in each of the above cases no suggestion is made that the required action on the proper object must result in the desired property at the requested time. The grounds upon which it is maintained that an imperative is not fulfilled are purely based on the denotative aspects of the agent's performance. Thus in none of the cases is it suggested that *because* the agent has, for example, acted with the wrong means he has come out with the wrong property at the wrong time. Cases 1. through 13. only illustrate the possible cases where the denotation of the agent's performance is not identical with the denotative aspects of the deatasized imperative. In themselves none of the above cases say anything about a *necessary relation* between say action upon an object and getting the desired result. The question as to the nature of such relations deal with the context or meaning of what is commanded, which is not a question proper for an extensional analysis.

Having set down the conditions under which an imperative is said to be unsuccessfully performed, one can proceed with giving the notion of the agent's unsuccessful performance of a commanded imperative. Introducing the symbol '$\overline{\text{Prfm}}$' to express the pragmatic relation of unsuccessfully performing an imperative, one has :

(T4) $((M \text{ Con }^{t1+}A, I_s).$ $(A \text{ Prfm }^{t1+} \text{ to }^{tc} \text{ f,x,y,F,t}_c))\equiv$
$(A \overline{\text{Prfm}}^{tc}, \text{fxyFt}_c\text{', Com M t}).$

Theorem (T4) states where imperator M has conveyed at time $^{t1+}$ to agent A imperative sentence I_s *and* agent A has performed during time-span t_{l+} to t_c and action, upon some object, with some means, to effect some property, at some time t_c, is equivalent to agent A not successfully performing at time t_c the imperative 'fxyFt$_c$', as commanded by M at time t. However, *unlike* (T3), (T4) holds if and only if the designational aspects of agent's performance are *not identical* to the designation of the performance intended by the imperator in conveying I_s at A at time $_{t1+}$. Actually, Theorem (T4) is a concise means of expressing all the cases reviewed above in which the denotation of the commanded imperative is not found to be identical to the denotation of the agent's performance.

It may be argued that on the face of it there is no difference in what (T3) and (T4) express, and thus it may appear that one is using "successful performance" and "unsuccessful performance" in exactly the same way. To so argue, however, would be to disregard the stated stipulations which make (T3) and (T4) intelligible. For without saying in the case of (T3) that there is a designative identity between the conveyed imperative and the agent's performance, one could not say that he is expressing the successful performance of an imperative. The converse of the stipulation theorem (T3) makes possible the expression of "unsuccessful performance" in (T4). Thus the content of (T3) and (T4) are really quite different, when interpreted properly.

It is interesting to note that with the notions of "unsuccessful performance," one can now explain how a response an imperative is "incorrect." For if the designata of the different aspects of the response by the agent is not identical to the corresponding designative aspects of the performance intended by the imperator in giving the imperative, the agent's response is said to be incorrect. Furthermore, an important step has also been reached by the articulation of the notion of an "incorrect" response to an imperative. For from the point of view of developing a logic of imperative, one now has a clear objective sense in which to say that a response to an imperative may be either correct or incorrect. This will be of great importance in the next chapter, where the logic of imperatives will be presented in light of the insights reached by this extensional and pragmatic analysis of imperatives.

For the sake of simplicity one can refer to the notion of "responding" to an imperative as either the agent's successful performance of an imperative on the unsuccessful performance of an imperative, taken as an exclusive disjunction. Thus the symbol "Res" will stand for responding to an imperative in either one of the two ways indicated by the above disjunction. Symbolically,

$$((A \ Prfm \ I_s) \lor (A \ \overline{Prfm \ I_s})) \supset (A \ Res \ I_s).$$

The expression of the agent's response to I_s, in conjunction with the notation of commanding an imperative makes possible the defining of the all-important notion of "imperatival discourse." Thus using the symbol 'ImpD' to mean the reflexive relation of discoursing imperatively, following theorem is possible :

(T5) $((M \ Com^t \ A, \ 'fxyft_c').(A \ Res^{tc} \ I_s, \ Com \ M \ t)) \equiv$

(M ImpD^t to ^t_c A, I$_s$).

Theorem (T5) states that where imperator M commands at time t to agent A imperative 'fxyFt$_c$' *and* agent A responds at time t$_c$ to imperative I$_s$ as commanded by M at time t, is equivalent to M is discoursing imperatively with A during time-span t to t$_c$, about imperative sentence I$_s$.

Of paramount importance for (T5), and indeed for the entire discussion on the structure of imperative dialogue, is the role of time in its temporal ordering of the key relations which make up such dialogue. For without the distinction when M commands I$_s$ to A, and when A responds to M's imperative, no meaningful account of the extensional and pragmatic nature of such discourse is possible. Thus the element of time is that which sequentially structures different aspects of imperatival discourse.

A number of points should stand out as unique results of the above analysis of imperative dialogue. First, it is seen that imperatives, and responses to imperatives can be safely handled as sentences about language and its users. This result contradicts the dogmatic opinion of Nuel D. Belnap, Jr. who observes in *An Analysis of Questions* that imperatives are not "wholly" linguistic in that they "lead from linguistic behavior into nonlinguistic behavior—..." Thus he argues that a logic of imperatives is not accessible as is a logic of questions and answers, which deals more closely with statements.[213] The discussion on the structure of imperative discourse has shown, however, that both the commanding of imperatives and the response to imperatives can be handled sententially. The fact that the above discussion allows for the analysis of "performance" as a sentence clearly indicates that the agent's response to the imperative can be treated linguistically. Thus Belnap's objection to the possibility of arriving at a logic of imperatives has been overcome.

Furthermore, it has turned out that one can speak of a command as being genuine, and the response to the imperative as being either correct or incorrect. Thus one has arrived at a means by which to objectively determine the acceptability of commands and responses to commands. This result is of great importance in the following chapter, where the logic of imperatives will be articulated. It is enough to point out here, however, that a decision method is now available for imperatives, and responses to imperatives, where this was not the case before.

Finally, it is observed that this entire discussion on the extensional and pragmatic nature of imperative discourse is articulated only in terms of three basic notions : "commanding" (*diataso*), "acceptance," and "performance." All other notions discussed above are defined in terms of these three ideas. Thus one must appreciate the economy yet power of the extensional and pragmatic approach in its ability to express a great deal by means of simple notions.

6

A Logic of Imperatives

In so far as the writers discussed above have suggested how a logic of imperatives can be presented, the logic given whithin this chapter is presented also in a highly tentative way. What is new, however, is the foundation from which it is articulated. For it's departure from past attempts lies in the fact that it is based upon purely extensional considerations.

The preceding informal analysis of imperatives provides a groundwork for handling imperatives and responses to imperatives sententially. Thus from an extensional and pragmatic viewpoint, an imperative is regarded as a sentence about an imperator who arranges and brings about through uttering a command some action upon an object so that a property will result for that object at some time. Similarly, a response to an imperative is regarded as a sentence about an agent's performance in acting upon an object so as to effect some property on the object at a prescribed time. Here also it was seen that a response to an imperative is termed "correct" when it has the identical extension as an imperative sentence, for which it is meant as a response. Thus also a response to an imperative is said to be incorrect if it does not have the same denotatum as the imperative.

The aim of this chapter, therefore, is to state in a meta-logic a logic of imperatives and responses to them, as these are conceived in the first chapter of this part. Furthermore, this logic will be somewhat akin to that of David Harrah's, who in various works attempts to develop a logic of questions and answers as an "information matching game."[214] Unlike Harrah's attempt, however, the relation between imperator and agent is taken as that of two individuals (imperator and agent) matching performance, that is, the performance required by the imperator and the performance given by the agent.

More importantly, a logic of imperatival events will be presented as arising from the said logic of imperatives, and from some recently developed notions on physical events and the relations between such events. Finally, within this same chapter the adequacy of the logic enunciated in the first three sections shall be considered. This discussion will cover two points. First, consideration will be given to how the proposed logic deals with the emotive quality of imperatives, which proved a stumbling block for the intensionalists. Secondly, the issue of the nature of imperative inference will be discussed as it related to the above logic. In this way a clearer understanding will be attained of the extensional approach towards a logic of imperatives.

Section 1.   *The Logic of Imperatives*

As a first step towards presenting the logic of imperatives a brief characterization of the formal language L shall be given. These characterizations will be treated as assumptions L, and shall be referred to as 'LA' meaning language assumptions.

LA 1.   L has denumerably many constants 'a', 'b' 'c', .. , and denumerably individual variables 'x', 'x_1', 'x_2', 'x_3', ..., which range over individuals of a denumerably infinite domain.

LA 2.   L has the predicates 'F', 'G', 'H',..., of individuals which are non-logical predicates.

LA 3.   L has the truth-functional connectives of conjunction '.', disjunction 'v', negation '—', material implication ' ⊃', and material equivalence '≡'.

LA 4. L has the notion of universal and existential quantification, the latter being expressed by the existential quantifier 'Ⅎ'.

LA 5. L has the following punctuation marks : '('and')'.

LA 6. With the punctuation marks in LA5. the universal quantifier is given as (x).

LA 7. Individual variables and individual constants are called *terms*. Thus also where 'f' is a functional constant, that is, 'f' designates a function having individuals as arguments, and 'a', ..., 'a_n' are terms, then 'f (a, a_1 ..., a_n)' is a term. Also, 'f (a, a_1, ..., a_n)' designates the values which the designation of 'f' has for the n-tuple formed from the designata of 'a', 'a_1', ..., 'a_n' as arguments.

LA 8. Given that 't', 't_1', ..., 't_n' are terms '($t_1 = t_2$)' is a well-formed formula or wff, as is 'Ka', where 'K' stands for any non-logical predicate. Other examples of well-formed formulas are: '(A·B)', '(AvB)', '(A≡B)', '(A⊃B)', '(—A·B)', etc. etc.

LA 9. The wff '($t_1 = t_2$)' is *true* if and only if 't_1' and 't_2' have the same designation. 'F (t_i, ..., t_n)' is *true* if and only if the n-tuple formed from the designata of 't_i', ..., t_n' stands in the relation designated by 'F', etc. etc.

LA 10. Every wff is meaningful, that is, either true or false.

LA 11. An occurrence of a variable x in a wff A is a *bound* occurrence of that variable if and only if that occurrence is within some well-formed part of A, having the form '(x)A'. In the case where some occurrence of x in A is not bound, then the occurrence of x is a *free* occurrence of x in A.

LA 12. Wffs having free variables are ambiguously true or false, depending on the interpretation of their free variables. Wffs with no free variables are determinately true or false, and will be termed *sentences*.

LA 13. 'p is *A-true* (or analytically true) in L' means that 'p' is a logical theorem of L. 'p *A-implies* q' means that 'If p then q' is A-true in L. In a similar manner 'p' is said to be '*A-equivalent* to q' or 'A—false.'

LA 14.   L is *consistent* in the sense that not every wff of L is provable in L, in the sense that if wff A is provable, then —A is not provable.

Definition 1.   The sign '!' will stand for the *commanding* of an imperative to an agent by an imperator.   Recalling the informal analysis of imperative discourse in the preceding chapter, '!' refers to the ostensibly observable commanding of some imperative by an imperator M. Thus '!' incorporates all that the primitive 'Com' was found to accomplish in the previous chapter.   Essentially, '!' is employed as a convenient metalinguistic device, such that when it is prefixing a wff of L, it distinguishes that wff as an imperative in L.   Hence any other wff of L which expresses the same truth as the wff prefixed by '!', shall be taken as the direct response to that imperative. For example, 'Fa' would be the direct response to '!Fa'.

Definition 2.   Elemental imperatives are true sentences in the pragmatic meta-language, and are exemplified as follows (granting that 'K' is any non logical predicate) : '!Ka', '!(x)Kx', '!($\exists$x) Kx', etc. Elemental imperatives require that one and only one action is to be performed at one time by the agent on one object.   In the examples given of some forms of elemental imperatives, the constant 'a' designates and the variable 'x' ranges over the object to be acted upon, and the nonlogical predicate 'K' refers to the property the object is to have when they have been acted upon by the agent.   Examples of such imperatives are "Shut the window !", "Shut the door !", etc.

Of foremost importance at this juncture is the clarification of what is meant by a "direct response" to an imperative.   For though it can be easily stated that the form of a direct response to the imperative say !Ka is Ka, it is quite another thing to explain why Ka is so conceived. Here, however, no new groundwork need be developed, since the idea of a direct response has already been prepared in the previous chapter. Accordingly, Ka. is the direct response to !Ka because Ka is the end result of the agent's *performance* relative to the command, !Ka. More precisely, Ka is really the outcome of the agent performing: f,a,y,k,t. This means that the agent has performed action f on object a with means y to effect property k at time t. Recalling as well further aspects of the discussion on responses to imperatives, it is seen that Ka can be objectively determined as "correct" or "incorrect" relative to its denotata and the denotata of !Ka.

An issue related to that of the nature of direct responses to imperatives, and one which figures prominently in the defining of imperatives, is that of the notion of "action." As stated in *Definition 2.*, it is the idea that *one action* is to be performed by the agent which distinguishes the elemental imperative from other types of imperatives. However, what is means by an action? In the investigation of the extensional and pragmatic nature of imperatival discourse the notion of action was only summarily considered as the observable behavior of some agent toward an object. Here, however, some more specific remarks are necessary because of the importance of this idea in defining imperatives and responses to imperatives.

It is maintained, therefore, that an action is the objectively observable behavior of an agent with respect to one distinct object. Furthermore, what distinguishes one action from another is the *combined fact* of the agent's objective behavior towards the object and the fact that one and only one object is being acted upon by the agent. For it cannot by only the specific behavior of the agent which distinguishes one action from another, since it often happens that the same behavior is exhibited by the agent towards a number of objects. Thus, for example, someone may close a number of doors, though it would be imprecise to claim that his closing of these doors constitutes one action. Rather, it seems more clear to say that each case of the agent closing a door is in action. Thus where one commands someone to close a number of doors, he is really giving a number of commands in *conjunction*: Close door A, and Close door B, and Close door C, and...!

Definition 3. *A direct response to an elemental imperative* is a true sentence saying that what the elemental imperative requests is the case, such that sentences of the form: 'Ka', '(x) Kx', '(ᴲx) Kx', '-Ka', etc. are forms for direct responses to elemental imperatives, where 'K' stands for any nonlogical predicate. Examples of such direct responses are "The window is shut.", etc.

Definition 4. *Disjunctive imperatives* are sentences having forms such as: '!(Ka+Kb)', '!(Fa+Fb)', '!(((x)Ex)+ ((X)Gx))', '!((Ex)Fx)+(Ex(Gx)))', etc., where '+' stands for exclusive disjunction. Here also 'a', 'b', and 'K', 'F', and 'G' refer to the intended properties these objects are to have when acted upon. Examples of these disjunctive imperatives are "Shut the window or shut the door!", "Either shut all of the windows or shut all of the doors!", etc. Disjunctive imperatives require that one of two alternative actions be performed.

Definition 5. *A direct response to a disjunctive imperative* is a true sentence saying that one, and only one, disjunct of the disjunctive imperative is the case. Thus direct responses to such imperatives may have forms exemplified as follows: 'Ka', 'Kb', '(x) Kx', '(ᴲx)Kx', etc., where 'K' stands for any nonlogical predicate. Examples of such responses are (relative to examples given in Definition 4.): "The window is shut.", "All the doors are closed.", etc.

Definition 6. *Conjunctive imperatives* are sentences exhibiting forms such as: '!(Fa.Gb)', ,!(Ka.Kb)', '!(((x)Fx). ((x) Gx)))', etc. Conjunctive imperative requiring two actions are to be performed in conjunction by the agent within a given time. As above, 'a', 'b', designate objects and 'x' range over objects, and 'K', 'F', and 'G' refer to the properties of these objects. Examples of such imperatives are: "Shut the window and the door!", "Open both the door and the closet!", etc.

Definition 7. *A direct response to a conjunctive imperative* is a sentence stating that whatever is required by the conjunctive is the case. Thus forms of such direct responses are: '(Fa.Fb)', '(Ka.Kb)', '(((x)Fx). ((x) Gx)))', etc. Relative to examples given in Definition 6., examples of direct responses to conjunctive imperatives are: "The window and door are shut.", Both the door and closet are shut.", etc.

Definition 8. 'I' is an imperative if it refers to either an elemental, disjunctive, or conjunctive imperative form.

Definition 9. 'I' refers to a *genuine imperative* or to a command which does not imply the physically or technically impossible, if 'I' refers to an imperative which does not involve or imply a false universal, existential, disjunctive or conjunctive statement.

As was pointed out in the informal analysis of imperatives, a genuine command is one which involves that which is physically or technically possible. Conversely, where the commanding of an imperative implies the physically or technically impossible, then commanding in this case is nongenuine. Furthermore, it is the command as a relation between, imperator, the act of arranging through uttering some order, and the command itself, which is said to "imply" the physically or technically impossible. Thus also because the objectively determinable "relation" of commanding is taken as doing the implying, the sense of "implication" here being intended is identical to that of implication between indicatives. For one has a public means of determining whether the "command relation" is genuine or not, which in turn allows it to be a truth-functional antecedent or consequent in any ordinary implicational expression.

The idea of a "genuine" imperative is important for two reasons. First it is an idea which can be determined formally in L, since it arises from the truth or falsity of the statement implied by the commanding. For example, the command "!Close the door." implies the statement "there is a door to be closed," which if false, renders commanding in this case nongenuine. Secondly, the idea of a "genuine" imperative is applicable to imperatives alone, without encountering any of the semantical problems which a ward like "true" involves when applied to imperatives.

Directive (i) Let '^eI' stand for an elemental imperative.
Directive (ii) Let '^dI' stand for a disjunctive imperative.
Directive (iii) Let '^cI' stand for a conjunctive imperative,
Directive (iv) Let 'R' stand for a direct response to either ^dI, ^eI, or ^cI.

Definition 10. ^eI is a nongenuine imperative if it implies (in the sense explained) a false statement.

Definition 11. ^dI is a nongenuine imperative if it implies (in the above sense) a false disjunction.

Definition 12. ^cI is a nongenuine imperative if it implies (in the above sense) a false conjunction.

Theorem 1.1 :   If 'p' is a true statement, then '!p' is constructible as an imperative, '!p' is recognizable as being genuine in L, and 'p' is A-equivalent to a direct response to '!p'.

Proof :   Definition 1. gives the meaning of '!' as a metalinguistic device which enables one to distinguish or recognize forms of imperatives from forms of statements which are direct responses to imperatives. Definition 9. sets down the criteria for recognizing a genuine imperative in L. Finally, Definitions 3., 5., and 7. illustrate that a direct response to any kind of imperative is a sentence saying that what the imperative states is the case.

Theorem 1.2 :   All imperatives are meaningful, that is, either genuine or nongenuine.

Proof :   LA 10. states that every wff is meaningful in so far as the wff is either true or false. Definitions 2., 4., and 6. presented the forms of imperatives as sentences, which according to LA 13. are wffs with no free variables. Thus in so far as imperatives are given as wffs they are meaningful. However, the wffs which make up the forms of imperatives are not said to be true or false, but rather genuine or ingenuine, according to Definition 9.

Thus Theorem 1.2 illustrates that an imperative such as "Shut the door!" must either be genuine or ingenuine, if it is to be at all significant. For it makes no sense to say that the imperative "Shut the door!" neither implies or does not imply that there is a door which is to be shut.

Theorem 1.3 : All meaningful imperatives are consistent in L.

    Proof : LA 15. expresses the consistency of L as being able to prove wff A, but not being able to prove wff—A in L. By Definition 9. it is seen that an imperative is genuine in L if it does not assume false statements, and nongenuine if it does assume false statements. Thus in so far as it can be proven that an imperative is genuine or nongenuine, all meaningful imperatives are consistent in L.

Theorem 1.4 : Each true sentence of L is a direct response to at least one imperative.

    Proof : Definition 3., 5., and 7. state that only true sentences of L are direct responses to imperatives.

Theorem 1.5 : Some responses are direct responses to serve more than one kind of imperative.

    Proof : Definitions 3. and 5. show that a direct response may serve as a direct response

to an elemental imperative or a disjunctive imperative. It can also be seen that
one direct response may serve as a
direct response to a conjunctive or a
disjunctive imperative.

Examples of cases where Theorem 1.5 is operative are the
following. Where one has the elemental imperative "open the
window!" and the disjunctive imperative "Open the window
or close the door !", both imperatives can be satisfied by
the direct response "the window is open." In both of the
above imperatives it is assumed that the same window is
referred to, and that the window is to be closed at the same
time in both cases. Also, the conjunctive imperative
"Open the window and close the door !" and the disjunctive imperative "open the window and close the door,
or leave !" are two imperatives satisfiable by one direct
response : "the window is open and the door is closed."
Here also there is assumed an identity between agents, objects,
and time in the conjunctive and disjunctive imperatives. In
both these cases the exclusive disjunctive nature of disjunctive imperatives makes possible the fulfilment of both
elemental and disjunctive imperatives, and conjunctive and
disjunctive imperatives, by one direct response. For as
Definition 5. states, the fulfilment of one disjunct of such
imperatives fulfils such disjunctive imperatives.

Theorem 1.6 :   No direct response to an ^eI can serve as
a direct response to ^cI.

Proof :   By Definition 2. it is seen that an elemental imperative requires that one
action be performed on one object at
some time. On the other hand, by
Definition 6., two actions are to be performed in a conjunctive imperative.
Thus in no case can a direct response
to a conjunctive imperative serve as a
direct response to an elemental imperative and conversely.

As already stated in the explanation of the notion of "action" above, an action is distinguishable from some other action on the basis of the compound fact of the agent's observable behavior relative to the object, and that only one distinct object is being acted upon. Thus in the case where two actions are required by an imperator in a conjunctive imperative, one can have the case where the agent is to behave differently towards two distinct objects, or he is to behave in the same way towards two distinct objects, or he may be required to behave in two different ways towards the same object. There are the three possible ways in which two actions in conjunction can be required by a conjunction imperative.

Theorem 1.7 : If a direct response to ^eI satisfies as a direct response to a ^dI, then ^eI A— implies ^dI, but not conversely.

Proof : Given '^eI' is short for '!Fa', '^dI' is short for '!(Fa+Fb)', and direct response Fa, then (1) $(Fa) \supset (Fa+Fb)$ is true in L : LA 3., and Difinition 4.,

(2) $(Fa+Fb) \supset (Fa)$ is false in L: LA 3. and Definition 4.

Thus : $^eI \supset {^eI}$, but $^eI \subset {^eI}$.

Theorem 1.7 illustrates the formal relation of implication between elemental and disjunctive imperatives. For example, where in the above proof 'F' designates the act of finishing, and 'a' designates some particular article, while 'b' designates a particular book, then a direct response to the elemental imperative "Finish the article !" serves also as a direct response to the disjunctive imperative "Finish the article or finish the book !" Thus, because disjunctive imperatives are defined in terms of exclusive disjunction, it can be formally proven that the said elemental imperative implies the conjunctive imperative. However, also by the definition of a disjunctive imperative it is seen that a direct response to a disjunctive imperative constitutes the fulfilment of *either one* of the imperative's disjuncts. Thus a

direct response to a disjunctive imperative does not necessarily serve as a direct response to an elemental imperative.
It is plainly evident that the direct response "the book is
finished" does not serve as a direct response to the imperative "Finish the article !" Thus the latter imperative can
never be formally implied by the imperative "Finish the
article or finish the book !"

> *Theorem* 1.8 :   If a direct response to a disjunctive
> imperative also serves as a direct res-
> ponse to a conjunctive imperative, then
> the disjunctive imperative implies the
> conjunction imperative, and conversely.

> *Proof* :   Given '^dI' is short for '$!(Fa.Fb)+(Gc))$',
> '^cI is short for '$!(Fa \cdot Fb)$', and
> direct response : (Fa.Fb), then

> (1) $!((Fa.Fb)+(Gc)) \supset !(Fa.Fb)$ is
> true in L:LA 3. and Definition
> 6., and

> (2) $!(Fa.Fb) \supset !(Fa.Fb)+(Fc))$ is true
> in L:LA 3. and Definition 6.,

> Thus : $^cI \supset {}^dI$ and $^dI \supset {}^cI$.

Theorem 1.8 shows how disjunctive and conjunctive
imperatives may imply each other. For where one has the
disjunctive imperative "Finish the article and the book, or go
away!" and a conjunctive imperative "Finish the article and
the book !", then the direct response "the article and the
book are finished" satisfies both imperatives. Where there
is such a direct response then it can be shown that both
imperatives formally imply each other, after proper
instantiation.

Definition 13. *A complete response* to an imperative I is a
sentence 'p' such that (1) 'p' is a direct response to I, and
(2) (p.I) is not A—false in L, and (3) (p.I) A—implies
some non—A—true response to I.

In Definition 13, of a sentence being a complete response
to an imperative one has a refinement of the   definition

of the direct response to different kinds of imperatives. For where 'p' is the statement that all of what an imperative requires of an agent is brought about by the intended agent, then p is also a complete response to that imperative. The idea of "completeness" here comes to involve how the response can be determined as "correct" or "incorrect." 'p' is thus taken as the agent's total intended response to an imperative. Hence it is seen that the conjunction of the intended response p and the imperative I cannot be A-false if the sentence p is a correct response to I and the imperative I is genuine. Thus the second condition of Definition 13 is consistent with the idea that p is a direct response to I. Thus also the third condition indicates that if the conjunction of direct response p and imperative I is a true statement, then it does imply any false statement, much as incorrect response to I.

Definition 14.   *A partial response* to I is a sentence 'p', where :

(1) 'p' is not A-true, and

(2) (p.I) is not A-consistent, and

(3) (p.I) does not A-imply any non-A-true direct response to I and

(4) Some direct response to I is such that the direct response to I and I is A-consistent and A-implies p.

Definition 14. is illustrated by the following example. Where one has the command : "Give John the book and the pencil !", a partial response would be "John has the book..." The latter response could never serve as a response to the said imperative since satisfying one conjunct of a conjunctive imperative does not satisfy the conjunctive imperative. Thus in this case it can neither be said that John has the book or the pencil. For the command requires that John have *both* the book and the pencil. For this reason, since the book must be had in conjunction with the pencil, having only the book in John's possession is irrelevant to the command. Thus also the response :

"John has the book...", being incomplete in satisfying the imperative, cannot be analytically true. Also, therefore, conjunction of the partial response and the imperative cannot be consistent. For in order that a sentence be consistent in L. it must be provable as either true or false in L. However, because partial responses are incomplete sentences they cannot be shown to be either true or false. Neither can a partial response and an imperative imply a false direct response to the imperative, since the partial response is not true and not false because of its incompleteness. Finally, the direct response to the imperative in question, or "John has the book and the pencil.", and the imperative imply the partial response : "John has the book...," in so far as part of the direct R to the imperative is the fact of John's having the book.

Theorem 1.10 :   No imperative can have partial responses.

Proof ;   For a sentence to be a direct response to an imperative I, it must be a *true sentence*, by definitions 3., 5., and 7. Thus no response as that defined by Definition 14. can be a direct response to I.

Definition 15 I_2 is *dependent upon* I_1 if and only if there is some direct response R_2 to I_1, such that, where R_1 is a direct response to imperative I_1 :

(1) $(R_1.I_1.I_2)$ is A-consistent, *and*,

(2) R_2 is A-implied by $(R_1.I_1.I_2)$, and by I_2.[215]

Definition 15. accounts for cases where an imperative cannot be acted upon and fulfilled unless some other imperative has been satisfied. For example, where 'I_1' stands for 'learn to read !' and 'I_2' stands for 'Read the book!' and both I_1 and I_2 are true sentences and are directed to one and the same person, then the agent cannot act upon I_2 unless I_1 has been acted upon by him. Thus also it is seen where the response to I_1, and I_1 and I_2, is a true conjunction, it is also a conjunction consistent in L. Furthermore, the conjunction $(R_1.I_1.I_2)$ analytically implies that the agent carries out I_2.

Definition 16. The imperatives are *independent* if and only if neither is dependent on the other.

Definition 17. I_1 *response contains* I_2 relative to a true sentence p if and only if :

> (1) I_1 has at least one direct response R_1, *and*

> (2) every R_1 is such that p. R_1A-implies some R_2 of I_2.

Definition 17. explains the case where one response satisfies two imperatives. Thus where 'I_1' is the elemental imperative 'open the window!', and 'I_2' is the disjunctive imperative 'open the window or shut the door !', then by definition to open the window is a direct response to both I_1 and I_2. It is to be noted as well that the relation of an imperative being response contained by some other imperative does not involve the dependence of the former imperative to the latter imperative, as defined in definition 15.

Definition 18. Two imperatives are *satisfiably equivalent* relative to a true sentence p, if each imperative response contains the other relative to p.

Definition 18. explains how two imperatives can be said to be equivalent. For example, where one has the two imperatives "Close all the windows in the room !" and 'Make the room safe from fire!', one response, namely "all the windows in the room are closed", satisfies both imperatives. For in the case of the latter imperative, closing the room's windows is an action conducive to making the room safe from fire. Thus, relative to a sentence about what makes a room firesafe, both of the above imperatives are satisfiably equivalent to each other.

Theorem 1.11 :   The relation of being "dependent upon" is non-reflexive, nonsymmetric, and nontransitive.

Proof :   Definition 15.

A review of examples given in Definition 15. will easily illustrate how "dependence upon" cannot be a reflexive, symmetric, or transitive relation. Given the imperative "Read the book !" is dependent upon the imperative "Learn to read !", it is evident that to satisfy the latter imperative does not necessarily involve satisfying the former imperative. For one can learn how to read without reading the book which is referred to by the first imperative. Thus the relation of dependence is reflexive. Also the relation of "dependence" is non-symmetric in the sense that it is asymmetric. For again with respect to the examples of Definition 15., one reads said book *because* he has learned how to read. However, one cannot be said to be *learning* how to read because he reads some book. Finally, the relation of "dependence" is also nontransitive in the sense that it is intransitive. For example, if to learn how to read enables one to read some book, it does not follow that one is able to read some other book because he has read the preceding book. Rather, one is able to read the latter book because he has learned how to read. (In all cases where the relation of "dependence" is explained above, learning how to read is taken in sense of learning to read on an advanced level.)

Theorem 1.12 :   "Response contains," relative to p, is reflexive, asymmetric, and intransitive.

Proof :   Definition 17.

The relation of the "response containment" between two imperatives must be reflexive. For given the imperatives "Close the window!" and "Close the window or close the door!", then one response "the window is closed" satisfies both imperatives. However, in the above two cases it does not follow that the former imperative is satisfied if the door is closed. Thus it follows that the relation of "response containment" is nonsymmetrical. Finally, the relation of "response containment" is nontransitive, since nothing follows from the satisfaction of both of the above imperatives.

Theorem 1.13 : "Satisfaction equivalence" is a reflexive, symmetric and transitive relation.

Proof : Definition 18.

As stated in the definition of "satisfaction equivalence" two imperatives are so related only if one direct response totally satisfies both of them. Thus with respect to such a direct response these two imperatives must be identical. Hence the relation of "satisfaction equivalence" must be reflexive, symmetric, and transitive.

Prior to exploring the logic of imperatival events, it is both interesting and helpful to recapitulate what this logic of imperatives enables one to do with imperatives. In this way a sharper focus can be attained of the *usefulness* of the above calculus of imperatives.

First it is seen that theorems 1.1, 1.2, and 1.3 respectively provide for the construction of imperatives for some given situation , for the determination of the "meaningfulness" of the imperative so constructed, and for the consistency or provability of the imperative in L.

Secondly, this logic provides for a simple means of distinguishing between the *form* or *structure* of an imperative from some other sentence of L. For Definition 1. defines the symbol '!' in totally extensional and pragmatic terms, and proceeds to state that before any wff this symbol turns the wff into an imperative.

Thirdly, by means of the definitions for direct responses to imperatives (definitions 3., 5., and 7.) there is seen that to every imperative there corresponds some direct response.

Fourthly, the calculus makes possible the distinction between a complete and a partial response to an imperative by means of definitions 13. and 14. Thus one has a means of determining what constitutes a "proper" response to an imperative.

Fifthly, the logic illustrates some formal relations between imperatives generally, and between particular kinds of imperatives. For definitions 15:, 16., 17., and 18. set down how imperatives may relate to each other with respect to direct responses to such imperatives. Also theorems 1.7 and 1.8 illustrate the ways in which elemental, disjunctive, and conjunctive imperatives may relate to each other.

Finally, the above logic of imperatives provides a means of illustrating how a direct response to an imperative can be implied by a true sentence of L. For by use of the idea of A-implication in LA 14. and the three definitions of direct response, the implication of a direct response can be illustrated.

These six points touch upon only some of the major aspects of the calculus of imperatives. In reviewing them it is always well to keep in mind that as articulated the above logic deals only with the "forms" of imperatives. This is to say that the aim of this logic is to translate into formal terms the structure of sentences dealing with imperatives and direct responses to imperatives. In this respect it may be said that the logic is a further refinement of the extensional and pragmatic analysis of imperatives in the last chapter. Thus to question the adequacy of the logic thus far is to question either the extensional and pragmatic analysis which underlies the logic, or to question the correctness of the translation of imperative sentences into formal expressions of. In the latter case one becomes involved with matters of syntax. For if it can be shown that imperatives can be handled as well-formed formulas prefixed by '!', then all formal relations applicable to wffs are applicable to formalized imperatives. However, to show that imperatives can be treated formally as wffs requires that the semantic analysis of imperatives, considered extensionally and pragmatically, is correct. Thus it is seen how very important it is for the discussion on the extensional nature of imperatival discourse in the preceding chapter to be as objective and clear as possible.

Section 2. *The Logic of Imperatival Events*

The next step, which may be taken as an approach towards a logic of imperatives, is the formal treatment of imperatives and their direct responses as single formal entities (sense to be defined). The problem with developing the latter kind of logic lies not so much in relating it or articulating it to the above logic of individual imperatives, but in clearly defining what is the "thing" or "entity" over which special variables are to range, and in so doing to refer to "imperatival events."

As a preliminary step it appears best to examine the notion of "event" extensionally, and from there to proceed on to particular events, such as imperatival events. Discussions on the nature of events have been few, the most notable of which are those of Jaegwon Kim and Prof. Richard Martin's recent contributions. In general it is granted by both these writers that events cannot be treated like physical objects, in the sense that events are not said to physically occupy space or time. Rather events are said to occur within space and time. On the other hand, it does seem possible to treat events extensionally by reference to a certain number of particulars having some ostensible determinable relation to one another. The latter approach is briefly suggested by Kim in "On the Psycho-physical Identity Theory," and it is along similar lines that Prof. Martin presents his more precise analysis of events and event-logic in "Events, Histories, Physical Objects : Some Logico-Metaphysical Reflections."[216]

Kim notes that expressions such as " 'a's being F'," "b's being G,' " a standing in relation R to b," etc. are examples of "designating-expressions for events," where 'a' and 'b' refer to particulars, and 'F', 'G' and 'R' to properties and relations. Thus it is seen from a totally extensional viewpoint that events involve *ordered* particulars, properties, and/or relations. Thus also it is seen that the entire triple or quadruple indicated above as being ordered designates

an event.[217]   In his rendition Prof. Martin makes the variables 'e', 'e_1' 'e_2', etc., have events as their values. Without immediately entering into the logic of e-expressions, it
is important to see how Martin handles special kinds
of events.[218]

For example, the event of Brutus stabbing Caesar is
reduced first to its symbolic form where 'b' stands for
Brutus, 'S' for stabbing, and 'c' for Caesar, and then struc-
tured into the sentence 'b S c', which expresses that Brutus
stabs Caesar. Here Prof. Martin goes one step further by
indicating that the above symbolic expression does not as
yet express an event, in that it is not a *virtual ordered triple*,
such as '<b, S, c>'.   The latter expression is an *event-
predicate* according to Martin, where events are arguments for such predicates, such that :

$$'<b, S, c>e'$$

says that e is a Brutus-stabbing-Caesar event.[219]

The contributions of the above two writers form the
basis from which a logic of imperatival events can be laun-
ched.   The first objective; therefore, is the thorough explanation of the kind of event an imperatival event is.   Thus
from the informal analysis of imperatives in the preceding
chapter it was seen that the whole discourse involving
imperatives and responses to them dealt with an imperator
M, an agent A, a relation termed "imperatival discourse"
or ImpD, and an imperative sentence about doing 'Fa'.
Thus in setting up the event-predicate for imperatival events
one has the following ordered quadruple <M, ImpD, A,
'Fa'>, so that :

(i)   '<M, ImpD, A, 'Fa'>e'

says that e is a imperator M-discoursing-imperatively-
with-an-agent-A-about-doing-'Fa' event.   For simplicity,
the sentential function expressed by (i) shall be written as
'Ie', where 'I' stands for the event-predicate of e in (i).

With the above symbolization of an imperatival event
one can go on to illustrate the notions of "beforeness,"

"temporal overlapping," "local simultaneity," etc. with respect to such events. Prof. Martin defines these ideas in the article cited above from the point of view of physical events generally.[220] Thus, theorems about imperatival events will be given as based upon the notions developed in the above article.

However, prior to presenting the logic of imperatival events it is enlightening to consider what now constitutes the commanding of an imperative. It is recalled in the previous chapter that the commanding of an imperative was considered as a pragmatic relation between an imperator commanding (as *diataso*) an imperative to an agent at a certain time. This was held as a sentenial expression of the act of commanding. However, with the introduction of the idea of an imperatival event, one can proceed on to a richer definition of the assertion and satisfaction of !Fa. Accordingly,

'!Fa'$=_{df.}$ ($\exists e$) ($\exists M$) ($\exists A$) ($\exists t$) (M ImpD A, 'Fa', t $\cdot$<M, ImpD, A, 'Fa'>e) The above definition states that one commands !Fa if for some event e, and some imperator M and some agent A and some time t, imperator M discoursing imperatively with agent A about doing 'Fa' at time t constitutes the event-predicate of event e. Here it is seen that '!' now has a richer sense than that of being only expressive of the extensional and pragmatic relation of commanding. Thus it is towards the logic of imperatival events to which attention is now turned.

The first notion to be considered is that of "beforeness." This idea assumes that "local time" refers to the time for hypothetical observer who witnesses the imperatival event. Thus Prof. Martin defines one event being before another as :

Def. I. "e_1 B e_2 expresses that e_1 is before e_2 in the *Eigenzeit* or local time of the observer."[221]

Reviewing the logic of individual imperatives reveals that a relation analogous to that of "beforeness" as defined above has been touched upon. For the saying that one imperative is dependent upon another imperative (Definition 15.) one assumes that the dependent imperative is fulfilled at a later time than the imperative upon which it depends. Thus the dependence of two imperatival events may be defined as :

> *Definition* 19.   One imperatival event e_1 is *dependent* upon another imperatival event e_2 if e_1 contains one imperative which is dependent upon an imperative in e_2.

> *Postulate* I. $(e_1) (e_2) ((Ie_1.Ie_2) \supset ((e_2 \text{ Dep } e_1) \supset (e_1 \text{ B } e_2)))$

The above postulate says that for every event e_1 and every event e_2, if these are imperatival events, then that event e_2 is dependent upon event e_1 implies that event e_1 comes before event e_2.

It is recalled that in explaining Definition 15. it was shown that where 'I_1' stood for the imperative 'Learn to read !' and 'I_2' stood for the imperative 'Read the book !" that an agent cannot act upon I_2 unless he has fulfilled I_1. Thus it is seen that I_1 must be acted upon prior to I_2, and this serves as a means of temporally distinguishing I_1 from I_2. It is to be noted, however, that whereas in Definition 15. the notion of "dependence" was defined in terms of individual imperatives, Definition 19. deals with the temporal relation of dependence between imperatival events. A closer look at Definition 15. reveals that it defines the notion of "dependence" in terms of direct responses to imperatives. Thus, though not specified, Definition 15. also dealt with events in so far as it involved the relation between an imperative and some direct response to it.

A notion arising from the definition of "beforeness" is that of two events "overlapping temporally" with each other. Martin defines this latter notion as follows :

> Def. II.   "Event e_1 may then be said to *overlap temporally*, or *eigentzeitlich* or *in local time*, with event e_2 provided neither

bears B-relation to the other. 'e_1LTOe_2'
abbreviates '$(-e_1 \text{ B } e_2 \cdot -e_2 \text{ B } e_1)$'."[222]

An idea involving "temporal overlapping" is derived
from saying that the two imperatival events are temporally
overlapping if one imperatival event is not dependent upon
another imperatival event, and conversely. Thus the
following definition is offered.

> *Definition* 20.   Two imperatival events e_1 and e_2 are *not
> dependent* on each other if neither events
> contain imperatives which are dependent
> on imperatives of the other imperatival
> events.

> *Postulate* II. (e_1) (e_2) $((Ie_1 \cdot Ie_2) \supset (((-e_1 \text{ Dep } e_2) \cdot$
> $(-e_2 \text{ Dep } e_1)) \supset ((-e_1 Be_2) \cdot (-e_2 Be_1)))$

This postulate states that given e_1 and e_2 are both
imperatival events, then where e_1 is not dependent upon
e_2 and e_2 is not dependent upon e_1, implies e_1 is not
before e_2 and e_2 is not before e_1.

Postulate II. simply says that two imperatival events
overlap if neither one of these events are before each other.
This is the same as saying that two imperatival events are
overlapping if neither is dependent on the other. As referred to here the relation of overlapping is richer than that
of being determined only by temporal factors. For in the
context of imperatival events, the relation involves the full
range of activity employed to fulfil the imperatives of Ie_1
and Ie_2, and not only the time factor at which the imperatives are to be satisfied. Finally, Postulate II. is presented
loosely enough so that aspects of one imperatival event
overlap with aspects of another, though both events are not
said to overlap totally with each other. The latter type of
total overlapping is illustrated further on.

A notion arising from considering temporal overlapping
between events is how events may be the "local part of"
other events.   Martin defines the notion as follows.

> Def.   III.   "...event e_1 is a *local temporal part* of
> event e_2 provided   every event which

overlaps temporally with e_1 overlaps also with e_2.

'e_1 LTP e_2' abbreviates '(e) (eLTO e_1 $\supset e$LTOe_2)'.''[223]

Again going back to the logic of individual imperatives one finds a notion which can be taken as analogous to the definition of a notion relating physical events. For it is easily seen that the relation of "response containment" is analogous to "local temporal part of," once it is stated how imperatival events may response contain each other. The latter definition is given as follows.

> *Definition* 21. One imperatival event is said to *response contain* another imperatival event if and only if one imperatival event contains imperatives which response contain imperatives of the other imperatival event.

> *Postulate* III. (e_1) (e_2) $(Ie_1.Ie_2) \supset (((e_1$ Res Con $e_2) \supset$
> $((e)(e$ LTO $e_1 \supset e$ LTO $e_2)))$

The above postulate states that for every event e_1 and $_-e_2$, where e_1 and e_2 are both imperatival events, then e_1 response contains e_2 if for every event e, e is a response forming a local temporal part of e_1 implies that e is a response forming a local temporal part of e_2.

The response containment between imperatival events is equivalent to these same events being the local temporal part of one another is best illustrated by a concrete case. Employing the examples used to illustrate containment between imperatives, one can say that the imperative "Account for the three stages of geologic change!" response contains the imperative "Account for the different phases of diastrophism!" All that response containment means in this case is that to fulfil the imperatives of the first kind includes fulfilling the imperatives in the latter kind. Extending this on to the level of events one would say that for an agent to act on all the imperatives of the latter kind,

so that one may look upon the fulfilment of each imperative of this group as so many events, means that these latter
events are a determinable part of the range of events making
up the fulfilling of the imperatives of the larger former
kind. Furthermore, the reason why the former sequence
of event is countable as part of the latter larger sequence
of events is because both kinds of imperatives require in
some cases the same responses.

As founded upon the idea of "local temporal part of"
the notion of two events being "simultaneous" is defined
as:

Def. IV.   "An event e_1 is locally simultaneous
                     with event e_2 provided every locally
                     temporal part of e_1 is a part of e_2 and
                     conversely. Thus 'e_1 Simul e_2' abbr-
                     eviates '(e) $(e$ LTP $e_1 \equiv e$ LTP$e_2)$."[224]

The notion of the "simultaneity" of two events may be
expressed in terms of the satisfaction equivalence of the
imperatives of two events. First, however, the definition
of how two imperatival events may be satisfiably equivalent should be presented.

Definition 22.   Two imperatival events are *satisfiably*
                     equivalent if all the responses to the
                     imperatives of one event are the same
                     as all the responses to the imperatives
                     of the other imperatival event.

Postulate IV. (e_1) (e_2) $(($Ie_1. I$e_2) \supset (($ e_1 Sat. Equ.$e_2) \supset$
                     $(($e$)$ (e) $(e$ LTP $e_1 \equiv e$ LSP $e_2)$ $)$ $)$

Postulate IV. states that for every e_1 and e_2, where e_1
and e_2 are both imperatival events, implies e_1 is satisfiably
equivalent to e_2 then e_1 is simultaneous with e_2.

The above postulate provides a means of expressing the
complete or total overlapping between two imperatival
events. This is in contrast to the partial overlapping expres-

sed by Postulate III. It may be noted as well that once
it is granted that one event is the LTP of another event is
equivalent to the first event response containing the second
event, then one must grant that if one event is simultaneous
with another event these two events are also satisfiably
equivalent, if they are imperatival events. That this follows
arises simply from the fact that the notions of "simultaneity" and "satisfaction equivalence" are respectively defined
in terms of "local temporal part" and response containment."

The last notion regarding how events are related is that
of two events being "discrete." Martin defines this notion
accordingly,

> Def. V. "...   the event e_1 is discrete from e_2 provi-
>   ded they occur at different times or in
>   different places..."[225]

An eqivalent notion with respect to imperatival events
is where such events have imperatives which are independent of imperatives in other imperatival events. The notion
of independence has been defined in Definition 16. Thus

> Definition 23.   Two imperatival events are totally
>   independent of each other if all the
>   imperatives of one such event are
>   independent of all the imperatives of
>   the other event.

Martin uses the symbol '/' to designate the relation of
"discreteness" between events. Prior to using this symbol
in interrelating the two immedite definitions, it is important
to point out that "discrete" events means that none of the
relations expressed by Def. I through IV. hold. Also, two
imperatival events are independent of each other if none of
the relations defined in Definition 19. through 22. hold between two imperatival events. Thus:

> Postulate V. (e_1) (e_2) ($(Ie_1 . Ie_2) \supset$ ((e_1 indep e_2)
> $\supset (e_1/e_2)$)

The above postulate says that for every e_1 and e_2,

where e_1 and e_2 are imperatival events, then if e_1 is independent of e_2, e_1 is discrete from e_2.

Some simple theorems of the logic of imperatival events may now be presented. Before their being brought forth, however, the following symbolism is needed.

Directive (v) Let '^{e}Ie' stand for an elemental imperatival event. This is an event involving an elemental imperative and its direct response.

Directive (vi) Let '^{d}Ie' stand for a disjunctive imperatival event. This is an event involving a disjunctive imperative and a direct response to one of the disjuncts of the imperative.

Directive (vii) Let '^{c}Ie' stand for a conjunctive imperatival event. This is an event which involves a conjunctive imperative and a direct response to a conjunctive imperative.

Theorem 3. 1: Any kind of imperatival event is before some other imperatival event.

Proof: *Postulate* I expresses the relation of implication between "beforeness" and "dependence." However, the dependence between imperatival events, as defined in Definition 19., is based upon the definition of "dependence" for individual imperatives, as set down in Definition 17. In this last definition it is stated that because one imperative is dependent on another, it in no way follows that only one kind of imperative can be dependent on some other kind of imperative. Thus the relation of "beforeness" which in Theorem 3.1 is said to be implied by "dependence," also does not presuppose that in the case of events only one kind of event can be before another kind of imperatival event.

Theorem 3.2 :   Any kind of imperatival event overlaps temporally with any other kind of imperatival event.

Proof :   Since Theorem 3.2 equates "overlapping" in terms of the relation of dependence, and the latter relation does not assume anything concerning the kind of imperatives which are involved, the nature of the imperatives which overlap is of no consequence.

Theorem 3:3 :   Where an elemental imperatival event ^eIe is the local temporal part of a disjunctive event ^dIe, the converse is not the case.

Proof :   In Theorem 3.1 "local temporal part" was equated in terms of response containment. Though Theorem 1.6 illustrates that one response may satisfy both an elemental and a disjunctive imperative, Theorem 1.8 shows that a disjunctive imperative is not implied by an elemental imperative, where both are satisfied by one direct response. Thus, in light of Definition 17., the direct response to the elemental imperative of the imperatival event does not imply, together with some true sentence p, the direct response to the disjunctive imperative in ^eIe. Hence the disjunctive imperatival event can never be part of an elemental imperatival event.

Theorem 3.4 :   Where ^eIe is the LTP of ^dIe, the converse is also true.

Proof : As in the above proof it is noted that LTP is defined in terms of response containment, of Definition 17. It is recalled that in Theorem 1.9, where R served as a direct response to ^{e}I and ^{d}I, then ^{e}I A-implies ^{d}I, and conversely. Thus where ^{e}Ie and ^{d}Ie, contain imperatives having common direct responses, one imperatival event ^{e}Ie A-implies the other ^{d}Ie, and conversely. Thus ^{e}Ie is a LTP of ^{d}Ie, and conversely.

Theorem 3.5 : No ^{e}Ie can ever be the LTP of ^{e}Ie, and conversely.

Proof : Theorem 1.7 shows that no direct response to an ^{e}I can serve as a direct response to a ^{e}I. Thus no relation of response containment can accrue between ^{e}I and ^{e}I, and thus no LTP relation can hold between events containing only one or the other of these imperatives.

Theorem 3.6 : ^{e}Ie may be Simul. with a ^{d}Ie.

Proof : Theorem 3.4. and 3.9.

Theorem 3.7 : Any kind of imperatival event may be discrete from any other kind of imperatival event.

Proof : In Theorem 3.5 "discreteness" is equated in terms of nondependence, and the absence of the LTP relation. The first condition of nondependence, however, does not limit "discreteness," to only some kinds of events, since the notion of "beforeness," on which it is partly based, does not apply only to some kind of imperatives, as Theorem 3.6 illustrates.

A notion resulting from the grouping of related events is the "total history" of an object. In the work cited, Martin explains that the history of a physical object is "the event consisting of *all* the events which "happen" to it." Thus he says that the event of Brutus stabbing Caesar is just one event making up the life or history of Caesar. Thus to every physical object there corresponds a unique event which is the total history of the object.[226]

It remains, therefore, to present the notion of a "history" of an object which involves imperatival events. However, prior to presenting this notion it is interesting to reflect upon the kind of object which is made up of a number of imperatival events. For physically tangible things like tables and chairs, as well as less tangible things like battles, victories, etc, can be said to result from some imperatival events. In the case of the latter one is still concerned with physical things, in so far as a battle, for example, partly involves a series of commands so as to effect adversity on an enemy. Yet one does not speak of a battle as he would speak of a chair. Though imperatival events may be said to *partly* make up both, it is easily seen that chairs have a definite concreteness which is lacking when one speaks historically of battles. All of this indicates that the objects whose histories are composed of imperatival events need not always be concretely physical objects.

The notion of a "history" with respect to imperatival events can be introduced very simply as the conjunction of a set of imperatives *and* the direct responses to the imperatives of the set. The notion of an imperative set can be presented as a number of imperatives which are ordered either with respect to some time factor or by means of the consequences of responding to the imperatives of the set. Thus the conjunction of an imperative set and all the responses to the imperatives of the set form the unique event known as the *imperatival history* of the object. What this means is that where one has to deal with an object which in some way results from someone giving someone else orders, then the conjunction of these orders and the agent's responses to them make up part of the history of the object. For example; supposing a master shows his apprentice how to make a chair by ordering him to cut the pieces for the chair such and such a length, etc. The conjunction of all the orders given by the master and all the responses of the agent make up the imperatival history of the chair. It may well be that the imperatival history of the chair does not constitute the "entire" history of the chair. For one may very well want to include within the chair's entire history what happens to it after it is made. However, it cannot be denied that "part of" the history of an object such as the chair is its imperatival history.

Following Martin's symbolization of histories of physical objects generally, it is held that where 'x' stands for some object, and '$y \ni y=y$' is a virtual class expression, then
(ii)   '$<x, y \ni y=y>e$'

states that e is the event of x's being self-identical, or a member of $y \ni y=y$. Event e may be thought of as making up all the events occurring to x at some time. In this way e comes to be a "slice" of the history of x.[227] Applying this expression to symbolize the notion of the imperatival history of an object, it is claimed that e makes up all the imperatival events of an object x. Accordingly, e would continue to represent a "slice" of the history of x, since it has already been pointed out that the imperatival history of an object forms part of the total history of an object.

Interestingly, none of the intensionalists discussed above even consider that there are three kinds of imperatives, that they exhibit some formal relations between each other, and that such a logic may serve as a means for dealing with imperative sets. Neither do these authors clearly consider the possibility that from the logic of individual imperatival events.

The logic articulated in the above two sections is of course useful in so far as it opens up new possibilities for pursuing the analysis of imperatives. It was seen in the examination of the literature on this issue that the contextualists had reached an impasse in their pursuit of a tenable logic of imperatives. For their attempts generally faltered when they tried to account for the relations between imperatives, and the possibilities for inferring one imperative from another. Thus by using a different approach, it is hoped that the extensional and pragmatic view of imperatives pushes back some of the menacing barriers for such a logic, and infuses new promise that a rational basis for value-theory is more accessible than otherwise thought.

However, the stated goal of this study is the investigation of why no acceptable logic of imperatives has yet to be devised, and to attempt to evolve such a logic on more plausible grounds. Thus, in so far as the criticism of the attempts by others is sound, and the proposed logic of imperatives is tenable, it is felt that the aim of this study has been met.

Section 3. *Comparisons and Contrasts*

Perhaps the most interesting feature of the logic presented in the last two sections is that there is never any question of *translating* imperatives into indicatives. It is recalled that ever since logics of imperatives have been attempted there has always been much argumentation as to how imperatives are going to be "reduced" to such and such an indicative, etc. However, the logic of imperatives of section 1, being based upon a conception of extensional pragmatics, is able to handle imperatives sententially with comparative case. The significance of this is that "inference" with respect to imperatives now is no different than inference in the ordinary two-valued propositional logic. Thus no new conceptions of inference need be introduced as has been the practice of the writers reviewed above. Because of this greater freedom to employ first order calculus, a simpler and more workable logic of imperatives results.

As a further indication of the greater workability of the proposed logic of imperatives, reference may be made to how an imperative, considered in an extensional and pragmatic sense, is rendered as a premiss in a valid syllogism. In the first section of this chapter the "genuine" imperative was formally defined as a well-formed formula prefixed by 'I', which did not imply some false indicative statement. Thus, given the imperative "close the door !" or '!Fa', where 'F' is the predicate of closing doors and 'a' names some door, this imperative is "genuine" where there is in fact a door to be closed. Thus it is seen that the idea of a "genuine" imperative is a notion which arises from the determination of the truth or falsity of an indicated state of affairs. Ordinarily, inference with respect to indicatives is held to be either "valid" or "invalid" depending upon the truth or falsity of the premisses or conclusions of a syllogism. Accordingly, in so far as imperative sentences are said to be genuine or nongenuine (in the sense discussed), they can also serve as premisses in valid (sound) syllogisms.

An example of such a syllogism is offered below, in which it is assumed that the imperative premiss is genuine and the response statement is true.

1. Imperator M commands that the door be closed at time t.
2. The agent A closes the door referred to by M at time t.

Therefore: The door which M commands to be closed is closed at t.

This syllogism is valid because premiss 1. is genuine, and premiss 2. is true. For as in the case where there is no reference to imperatives, it is impossible for the premisses of a *sound* syllogism to be true and the conclusion false. Thus also, in the above example, the conclusion is also true. Thus because of the identity in the nature of indicative and imperative inference, no special difficulty arises in having premisses which contain imperatives, in a valid syllogism. In previous attempts, however, a major topic of difficulty was how to include an imperative in the premisses or conclusions of a syllogism.

Interestingly, none of the intensionalists discussed above

even consider that there are three kinds of imperatives, that they exhibit some formal relations between each other, and that such a logic may serve as a means for dealing with imperative sets. Neither do these author clearly consider the possibility that from the logic of individual imperatives one can go on to a logic of imperatival events.

The logic articulated in the above two sections is of course useful in so far as it opens up new possibilities for pursuing the analysis of imperatives. It was seen in the examination of the literature on this issue that the contextualists had reached an impasse in their pursuit of a tenable logic of imperatives. For their attempts generally faltered when they tried to account for the relations between imperatives, and the possibilities for inferring one imperative from another. Thus by using a different approach, it is hoped that the extensional and pragmatic view of impera tives pushes back some of the menacing barriers for such a logic, and infuses new promise that a rational basis for value-theory is more accessible than otherwise thought.

However, the stated goal of this study is the investigation of why no acceptable logic of imperatives has yet to be devised, and to attempt to evolve such a logic on more plausible grounds. Thus, in so far as the criticism of the attempts by others is sound, and the proposed logic of imperatives is tenable, it is felt that the aim of this study has been met.

FOOTNOTES

1. Menger, Karl., "A Logic of the Doubtful, On optative and Imperative Logic," *Reports of a Mathematical Colloquium*, 2nd. Series, (1939), p. 58.

2. Mally, Ernst, *Grundgesetze des Sollens : Elements der Logic des Willens*, Graz, 1926, Leuschner & Lubensky, Universitats—Buchandlung, p. 1-2.

3. Brentano, Franz, *The Origin of the Knowledge of Right and Wrong*, English Translation, Cecil Hague, New York, E.P. Dutton & Co., 1902, p. 8-9.

4. Eaton, H.O., *The Austrian Philosophy of Values*, University of Oaklahoma Press, 1930, p. 44.

5. Eaton, H.O., pp. 44-45.

6. Brentano, Franz, pp. 10-11. (Here Brentano is seeking to point out the similarity between action directed towards the realization of an end, and rational action.)

7. Mally, Ernst., pp. 10-11.

8. Ibid., pp. 68-69

9. Ibid., p. 72.

10. Ibid., pp. 2-3.

11. Findlay, J.N., *Meinong's Theory of Objects and Values*, 2nd edition, Oxford at the Clarendon Press, 1963, p. 67.

12. Ibid., p. 67, and pp. 89-91.

13. Mally, Ernst. *Grundgesetze des Sollens*, pp. 2-3.

14. Ibid., p. 2.

15. Menger, Karl. pp. 57-58. (The proof which follows is an elaboration of Menger's laconic proof. The reasons for each step of the proof are given in double parenthesis, to the right of each deduction.)

16. Ibid., p. 58.
17. Ibid., p. 59.
18. Ibid., p. 59.
19. Ibid., p. 59.

20. Ibid., p. 59-60.
21. Ibid., p. 60.
22. Ibid., p. 53.
23. Kneale, W. & Kneale, M., *The Development of Logic*, Oxford at the Clarendon Press, 1964, pp. 574-575.
24. Menger, Karl, p. 55.
25. Carnap, Rudolf, *Philosophy and Logical Syntax*, 1935, Kegan Paul, p. 24.
26. Ibid., p. 25 and p. 103.
27. Carnap, "The Elimination of Metaphysics Through Logical Analysis of Language," in *Logical Positivism*, ed. by A.J. Ayer, the Free Press, 1960, Glencoe, Illinois, pp. 63-64.
28. Ibid., p. 77.
29. Schlick, Moritz, "What is the Aim of Ethics," in *Logical Positivism*, ed. by A.J. Ayer, The Free Press, 1960, Glencoe, Illinois, p. 263.
30. Ayer, A.J. *Language, Truth and Logic*, Dover Publications, Inc., pp. 107-108.
31. Stevenson, C.L. "The Emotive Meaning of Ethical Terms," in *Logical Positivism*, ed. by A.J. Ayer, The Free Press, Glencoe, Illinois, p. 269 and pp. 278-279.
32. Dubislav, Walter, "*Zur Ubergrundbarkeit der Forderungssatze*," Theoria, vol. 3 (1937), pp. 337-338.
33. Ibid., p. 339.
34. Ibid., pp. 340-341.
35. Jörgensen, Jorgen, "Imperatives and Logic," *Erkenntnis*, vol. 7, (1937-38), pp. 288-289. (This same opinion is voiced by Henri Poincare, in *Mathematics and Science* : Last Essays, translated by John W. Bolduce, Dover Publications, Inc., New York, 1963, p. 103).
36. Ibid., p. 289.
37. Ibid., p. 289.
38. Ibid., p. 291.
39. Ibid., pp. 292-298.
40. Ibid., p. 293.
41. Grelling, Kurt "Zur Logic Sollsatze," *Unity of Science Forum*, 1939, p. 44.
42. Ibid., pp. 44-45.
43. Ibid., p. 45.
44. Reach, K., "Some comments on Grelling's paper "Zur Logic der Sollasatze," review, *Journal of Symbolic Logic*, vol. 5, (1940), p. 39.
45. Grue-Sorensen, "*Imperativsatz und Logik. Begegnung einer Kritik*," Theoria, vol. 5, (1939), pp. 197-198.

46. Sorainen, Kalle, *"Der Modus und die Logic," Theoria*, vol. 5, (1939), p. 203.

47. Hofstadter A. & McKinsey, J.C.C., "On the Logic of Imperatives," Philosophy of Science, vol. 6, (1939), p. 446.

48. Ibid., p. 447.

49. Carnap, Rudolf, *The Logical Syntax of Language*, London : Kegan Paul, 1937, pp. 2-4.

50. Hofstadter, A., & McKinsey, J.C.C., p. 447.

51. Ibid., p. 448,

52. Ibid., p. 448.

53. Ibid., p. 449.

54. Ibid., p. 449.

55. Ibid., pp. 449-450.

56. Ibid., p. 451.

57. Ibid., p. 451.

58. Ibid., p. 452.

59. Ibid., pp. 453-454.

60. Beardsley, E.L., "Imperative Sentences in Relation to Indicatives," *Philosophical Review*, vol. 53, (1944), p. 175.

61. Ibid., p. 175.

62. Beardsley, E.L., "The Semantical Aspect of Sentences," *Journal of Philosophy*, XL, (1943), p. 393,

63. Ibid., pp. 394-395.

64. Ibid., pp. 396-397.

65. Beardsley, E.L., "Imperative Sentences in Relation to Indicative," pp. 178-179.

66. Ibid., pp. 179-180.

67. Ibid., p. 180.

68. Ibid., p. 179.

69. Ibid., p. 183.

70. Cherry, Colin, *On Human Communication*, MIT Press, Cambridge, Mass., p. 221.

71. Beardsley, E.L. "Imperative Sentences in Relation to Indicatives," p. 176.

72. Ibid., p. 177.

73. Ibid., pp. 180-181.

74. Ibid., p. 181.

75. Ross, Alf, "Imperatives and Logic," *Philosophy of Science*, Volume 11, 1944. pp. 30-31.

76. Ibid., p. 31.

77. Ibid., pp. 32-33.

78. Ibid., pp. 33-34.

79. Ibid., p. 35.

80. Ibid., pp. 35-36.

81. Ibid., p. 43, and p. 45.

82. Ibid., pp. 38-39.

83. Ibid., p. 39.

84. Ibid., p. 40.

85. Ibid., p. 40.

86. Ibid., p. 40.

87. Ibid., pp. 42 and 43.

88. Bohnert, H.G., "The Semantic Structure of Commands," *Philosophy of Science*, v. 12, (1945), pp. 302-303.

89. Ibid., pp. 303-304.

90. Ibid., p. 305.

91. Ibid., p. 306.

92. Ibid., p. 306.

93. Ibid., p. 307.

94. Ibid., pp. 309-310.

95. Ibid., pp. 311-312.

96. Ibid., p. 312.

97. Ibid., p. 312.

98. Ibid., pp. 312-313.

99. "Imperative Sentences," *Mind*, (1949), vol. LVIII, p. 22.

100. Ibid., "Imperative Sentences," p. 22.

101. Ibid., p. 25.

102. Ibid., p. 27.

103. Toulmin, S.E. & Baier, K., "On Describing," in *Philosophy and Ordinary Language*, edited by Charles E. Caton, University of Illinois Press, Urbana, 1963, pp. 203-204.

104. Hare, R.M., Imperative Sentences," pp. 27-28.

105. Ibid., p. 28.

106. Ibid., *The Language of Morals*, p. 18.

107. Ibid., "Imperative Sentences," p. 31.

108. Turnbull, R.C., "A Note on Mr. Hare's "Logic of Imperatives,"" *Philosophical Studies*, (1954), vol. 5, pp. 34-35.

109. Hare, R.M., "Imperative Sentences," pp. 31-32.

110. Peters, R.F., "R.M. Hare on Imperative Sentences," *Mind*, vol. 58, (1949), pp. 538-539.

111. Ibid., pp. 539-540.

112. Duncan-Jones, A., "Assertions and Commands," *Proceedings of the Aristotelian Society*, vol. 5,2 (1952), pp. 200-201.

113. Ibid., pp. 201-202.

114. Ibid., p. 201.

115. Popper, K.R., *The Open Society and its Enemies*, vol. 1, Kegan Paul, London, 1945, p. 53.

116. Ibid., 204-205.

117. Ibid., p. 205.

118. Prior, A.N., *Logic and the Basis of Ethics*, Oxford University Press, (1949), pp. 71-72.

119. Strawson, P.F. "Truth," in *Truth*, edited by G. Pitcher, Engelwood Cliffs, N.J., (1964), pp. 40-42.

120. Castaneda, Hector Neri, "*Un Sistema General de la Logica Normativa*," *Dianoia*, (Mexico), vol. 2 (1957), p. 304.

121. Ibid., "A Note on Imperative Logic," *Philosophical Studies*, vol. 1, no. 1,, (1955), pp. 2-3, "*Un Sistema General de la Logica*," p. 305., "Imperative Reasonings," *Philosophy and Phenomenological Research*, vol. 21, (1960), p. 38, and "Imperatives, Decisions, and Oughts," in *Morality and the Language of Conduct*, edited by H.N. Castaneda and G. Naknikian, Detroit, Wayne University Press, 1965, pp. 264-266.

122. Ibid., "A Note on Imperative Logic," p. 1-2.

123. Ibid., p. 2.

124. Ibid., p. 3.

125. Ibid., p. 3.

126. Ibid., p. 3.

127. Ibid., "*Un Sistema General de la Logica Normativa*," pp. 304-305.

128. Ibid., p. 305.

129. Ibid., pp. 306-307.

130. Ibid., p. 307.

131. Ibid., p. 308.

132. Ibid., pp. 308-309.

133. Ibid., "Imperative Reasonings", pp. 23-24,

134. Ibid., "*Un sistema General de la Logica Normativa*," p. 309.

135. Ibid., pp. 308-309.

136. Ibid., p. 309 (It is necessary to present Castaneda's logic in its entirety because as a logic it must be looked upon as a whole, and not in disjointed parts.)

137. Ibid., pp. 310-314.

138. Ibid., pp. 310-313.

139. Stahl, Gerold, *"Nota sobre la logica de los finesy medios," The Journal of Symbolic Logic*, (1957), p. 87.

140. Castaneda, Hector-Neri, "Imperatives, Decisions, and 'Oughts,'" pp. 270-271.

141. Ibid., p. 279.

142. Von Wright, George H., *Norm and Action*, Routledge and Kegan.

143. Ibid., pp. 2-5.

144. Ibid., p. 129.

145. Ibid., pp. 35-36.

146. Ibid., pp. 17-22.

147. Ibid., pp. 28-29.

148. Ibid.. pp. 29-30.

149. Ibid., pp. 30-31.

150. Ibid,, p. 34.

151. Ibid., p. 34.

152. Ibid., p. 308.

153. Ibid., pp. 42-43.

154. Ibid., p. 43.

155. Ibid., p. 45.

156. Ibid., pp. 46-47.

157. Ibid., pp. 48-49. (The following table presents four conditions under which one can either act or forbear to act. Thus in the first case if one acts to preserve pTp, then p will remain. If, on the other hand, one forbears to preserve pTp, then p is no longer present.)

158. Ibid., pp. 60-61.

159. Ibid., p. 60.

160. Ibid., p. 58.

161. Ibid., p. 61.

162. Ibid., p. 59.

163. Ibid,, pp. 60-61.

164. Ibid., p. 60-61.

165. Ibid., p. 61.

166. Ibid., p. 61.

167. Ibid., p. 61-62.

168. Ibid., p. 62.

169. Ibid., p. 135.

170. Ibid., pp. 94 and 134-315.

171. Ibid., p. 133.

172. Rescher, Nicholas, *The Logic of Commands*, Dover Publications, 1966, New York, p. 3.

173. Ibid., p. 72.

174. Ibid., pp. 77-78.

175. Ibid., p. 53.

176. Ibid., pp. 63-64.

177. Ibid., pp. 68-69. (Here also it is necessary to go into detail, since the issue at hand is involved and cannot be roughly summarized without doing injustice to the author.)

178. Ibid., p. 79.

179. Ibid., p. 79-80.

180. Ibid., p. 79-80.

181. Ibid., p. 89.

182. Ibid., p. 75 and 89.

183. Ibid., p. 7.

184. Williams, B.A.O., "imperative Inference," *Analysis Supplement*, (1963, for vol. 23), pp. 30-31. (see also Peters' view p. 114, above).

185. Rescher, N. and Robinson, J., "Can One Infer Commands From Commands ?" *Analysis*, vol. 24, (1964), pp. 176-177.

186. Gombay, Andre, "Imperative Inference and Disjunction," *Analysis*, vol. 25, p. 61.

187. Simon, Herbert A., "The Logic of Rational Decision," *The British Journal for the Philosophy of Science*, Vol. XVI, Nov. 1965, No. 63, p. 170; "The Logic of Heuristic Decision Making," in *The Logic of Decision and Action*, N. Rescher, ed., University of Pittsburgh Press, 1967, pp. 1-2; *The Sciences of the Artificial*, The M.I.T. Press, 1970, p. 22.

188. Ibid., "The Logic of Rational Decision," p. 170 and p. 179. "The Logic of Heuristic Decision Making," p. 1.

189. Ibid., "The Logic of Heuristic Decision Making," p. 2, *The Sciences of the Artificial*, pp. 4-5.

190. Ibid., "The Logic of Heuristic Decision Making," pp. 3-4, and p. 6.

191. Davidson, Charles H. and Koenig, Eldo C., *Computers*, John Wiley and Sons, Inc., 1967, p. 320 and p. 503.

192. Gardner, Martin, *Logic Machines, Diagrams and Boolean Algebra*, Dover Publications, Inc., New York, pp. 142-143.

193. Simon, H.A., "The Logic of Rational Decision," p. 173, The Science of the Artificial, pp. 59-62.

194. Ibid., *The Science of the Artificial*, p. 62.

195. Ibid., "The Logic of Heuristic Decision Making," pp. 7-8.

196. Ibid., "The Logic of Heuristic Decision Making," p. 7. "The Logic of Rational Decision," p. 183.

197. Ibid., "The Logic of Heuristic Decision Making," pp. 9-10, "The Logic of Rational Decision," pp. 180-181.

IMPERATIVES AND THEIR LOGICS

198. Ibid., "The Logic of Heuristic Decision Making," p. 12, *The Sciences of the Artificial*, pp. 66-69.

199. Ibid., "The Logic of Heuristic Decision Making," p. 12.

200. Ibid., pp. 15-16.

201. Ibid., pp. 15-16.

202. Davidson, C.H. and Koenig, E.C., *Computers*, pp. 13-15.

203. Ibid., pp. 324-325.

204. Keene, G.B., "Can Commands Have Logical Consequences?" *American Philosophical Quarterly*, vol. 3, (1966), p. 63.

205. Quine, Willard Van Orman, *From A Logical Point of View*, Second edition, Harper & Row, New York, 1961, pp. 130-131.

206. Lewis, C.I., "The Modes of Meaning," in *Semantics and the Philosophy of Language*, edited by L. Linsky, Univ. of Illinois Press, 1952. p. 238.

207. Ibid., "The Modes of Meaning," p. 238.

208. Wittgenstein, Ludwig, *Philosophical Investigations*, trans. by G.E.M. Anscombe, 3rd ed. McMillan Co., 1970. p. 82 e.

209. Liddell and Scott, *A Lexicon*, (Abridgement), Oxford at the Clarendon Press, 1963, p. 167.

210. Martin, Richard M., *Performance*, mimeograph copy of this monograph, pp. 7-8.

211. Ibid., p. 6-7. (It is important to point out that the above formula (4) is an adaptation of Prof. Martin's formalization of the notion of "performance." Also, 'Prfm' is taken as involving the simplest kinds of action-types, which are "physical motions or physico-chemical Processes." Such action-types are expressed by the variable 'f' in (4).)

212. In reading these tables it should be kept in mind that the action referred to by 'f' is that alluded to in the imperator's commanded imperative, whereas the action referred to by 'f²' is that of the agent's performance. In the same way 'x¹' and 'x²' are to be read, etc.

213. Belnap, Jr., Nuel D., *An Analysis of Questions : Preliminary Report*, Technical Memorandum, System Development Corporation, 2500 Colorado Ave., Santa Monica, California TM-1287/000/00, p. 10.

214. Harrah, David, "A Logic of Questions and Answers," *Philosophy of Science*, v. 28., no. 1, 1961, and *Communication : A Logical Model*. M.I.T Press, 1963.

215. Ibid., "A Logic of Questions and Answers," pp. 42-45. (The notions developed by Harrah, that is, "partial response," "complete response," "response containment," etc., are taken by him in the context of questions and answers to questions. Here, however, these notions are employed in a framework different from that envisioned by Harrah. Thus, where necessary these ideas are modified to accommodate imperatival discourse.)

216. Kim, Jaegwon, "On the Psycho-physical Identity Theory" *American, Philosophical Quarterly*, vol. 3, 1966.

    Martin, Richard M., *Events, Histories, Physical Objects : Some Logico-Metaphysical Reflections*, (mimeograph copy).

217. Kim, Jaegwon, "On the Psycho-physical Identity Theory," pp. 231-232.

218. Martin, Richard M., *Events, Histories, Physical Objects : Some Logico-Metaphysical Reflections*, pp. 9-10.

219. Ibid., p. 11.

220. Ibid., pp. 9-10.

221. Ibid., p. 9.

222. Ibid., p. 9.

223. Ibid., p. 9.

224. Ibid., p. 9.

225. Ibid., pp. 7-8.

226. Ibid. p. 11.

227. Ibid., p. 12.

BIBLIOGRAPHY

1. Anderson,   *The Formal Analysis of Normative System:*
   Alan, R.   Technical Report no. 2, U.S. Office of
                    Naval Research, Contract SAR/Non R,
                    609 (16), 1956.

2. Aqvist, Lennart "Deontic Logic Based on a Logic of
                    'Better'", *Acta Philosophia Fennica* fasc.
                    16, (1963).

3. Ibid.   "Interpretations of Deontic Logic," *Mind*,
                    vol. 73 (1964).

4. Ibid.   "Choice-Offering and Alternative-Present-
                    ing Disjunctive Command", *Analysis*, vol.
                    25, (1965).

5. Austin, J.L.   *Philosophical Papers*, ed. J.O. Urmson
                    and G.J. Warnock, Oxford, 1961, Claren-
                    don Press, Oxford.

6. Ibid.   "Performative-Constative," in *Philosophy
                    and Ordinary Language*, ed. by Charles E.
                    Caton, University of Illinois Press, Ur-
                    bana, 1963.

7. Ayer, Alfred J. *Language, Truth and Logic*, Dover Publi-
                    cations, Inc. New York, (1961).

8. Bar-Hillel,   "Semantic Information and its Mea-
   Yehoshua   sures," in Heinz von Foerster. ed., *Cyber-
                    netics Circular, Causal and Feedback
                    Mechanism in Biological and Social Sys-
                    tems*, Transaction of the Truth Confer-
                    ence, April, 1953, Princeton, New Jersey.

9. Ibid.   "An Examination of Information Theory," *Philosophy of Science*, vol. 22, no. 2, 1955.

10. Ibid.   "Logical Syntax and Semantics," *Language* 30, no. 2, April-June, 1954.

11. Beardsley, E.L. "Imperative Sentences in Relation to Indicatives," *Philosophical Review*, vol. 53, (1944).

12. Beth, E.W.   "On a possible Interpretation of Imperatives," *Synthese*, vol. 5, (1946-1947).

13. Bohnert,   "The Semiotic Status of Commands,"
    Herbert G.   *Philosophy of Science*, vol. 12, (1945).

14. Brentano, F.C. *The Origin of the Knowledge of Right and Wrong*, English Translation by Cecil Hague, New York, F.P. Dutton & Co., (1902).

15. Carnap,   *The Logical Syntax of Language*, Har-
    Rudolph   court, Brace and Co., New York, (1937).

16. Ibid.   *Introduction to Semantics*, Harvard University Press, (1942).

17. Ibid.   "Modalities and Quantifiers," *Journal of Symbolic Logic*, vol. XI, (1946).

18. Ibid.   *Meaning and Necessity*, University of Chicago Press, (1947)

19. Ibid.   "On Some Concepts of Pragmatism", *Philosophical Studies*, VI, (1955).

20. Castaneda,   "Logica de las normas y la etica," *Uni-
    Hector, Neri   versidad de San Carlos*, vol. 30, (1954).

21. Ibid.   "A Note on Imperative Logic," *Philosophical Studies*, vol. 6, 1955.

22. Ibid.   "Un Sistema general de la logica normativa." *Dianoia*, (Mexico), vol. 2, (1957).

23. Ibid.   "Imperatives and Deontic Logic," *Analysis*, vol. 19, (1958).

24. Ibid.   "Outline of a Theory of the General
                          Logical Structure of the Language of
                          Action," *Theoria*, vol. 26, (1960).

25. Ibid.   "Imperative Reasoning," *Philosophy and
                          Phenomenological Research*, vol. 21,
                          (1960-1961).

26. Ibid.   "A logico-Metaphysical Inquiry into the
                          Language of Action," *Morality and the
                          Language of Conduct*, ed. by G. Nakni-
                          kian and H. Castaneda, Detroit, Wayne
                          University Press, 1962.

27. Cherry, Colin   *On Human Communication*, The Techno-
                          logy Press and John Wiley & Sons, Inc.,
                          Cambridge, Mass., (1957).

28. Chisholm, R.   "Contrary-to-Duty Imperatives and De-
                          ontic Logic," *Analysis*, vol. 24, (1963).

29. Cohen,   *Reason and Nature*, Harcourt, Brace and
    Morris R.   Co. New York, (1931).

30. Downing, P.F.   "Opposite Conditionals and Deontic
                          Logic," *Mind*, vol. 70 (1961).

31. Dubislav,   "Zur Unbergrundbarkeit der Forderungs-
    Walter   satze," *Theoria* vol. 3, (1937).

32. Duncan-Jones,   "Assertions and Commands," *Proceedings
    A.E.   of the Aristotelian Society*, vol. 52 (1952)

33. Edwards, Paul   *The Logic of Moral Discourse*, Glencoe
                          Press, New York (1955).

34. Erdmann,
    Brenno   *Logic*, vol. 1, Halle, a.s. 1907.

35. Ewing, A.C.   *The Definition of the Good*, London and
                          New York, 1947.

36. Field, G.C.   "Note on Imperatives," *Mind*, vol. 59
                          (1950).

37. Fisher, Mark   "A Logical Theory of Commanding,"
                          Logique et Analyse, vol. 4 (1961).

38. Ibid.   "A System of Deontic-Alethic Modal
                          Logic," *Mind*, vol. 71, (1962).

39. Frege, G.   "On Sense and Nominatum," in *Readings in Philosophical Analysis*, ed. by H. Feigl and W. Sellars, Appleton-Century-Crofts, Inc., (1949).

40. Geach, Peter T.   "Imperative Inference, *Analysis Supplement*, 1963, (vol. 23).

41. Ibid.   "Imperatives and Deontic Logic," *Analysis*, vol. 18 (1958).

42. Gibbons, P.C.   "Imperatives and Indicatives," *Australasian Journal of Philosophy*, vol. 38 (1960).

43. Gombay, Andre   "Imperative Inference and Disjunction," *Analysis*, vol. 29, (1965).

44. Grelling, Kurt   "Zur Logik des Sollsatze," *Unity of Science Forum*, January, 1939.

45. Grue-Sorensen, K.   "Imperativsatze und Logik, Begegnung einer Kritik," *Theoria*, vol. 5, (1939).

46. Hamblin, C.L.   "Questions," *The Australasian Journal of Philosophy*, vol. 36, (1958).

47. Hare, R.M.   "Imperative Sentences," *Mind*, vol. 58 (1949).

48. Ibid.   "An Examination of *The Place of Reason in Ethics* by S.E. Toulmin," *Philosophical Quarterly*, vol. 3, (1951).

49. Ibid.   *The Language of Morals*, Oxford 1952, reprinted 1961.

50. Ibid.   *Freedom and Reason*, Oxford, 1963.

51. Ibid.   "Some Alleged Differences between Imperatives and Indicatives," *Mind*, vol. LXXVI, no. 303, July, 1967.

52. Harrah, David   "The Adequacy of Language," *Inquiry*, 3, (1960).

53. Ibid.   "A Logic of Questions and Answers," *Philosophy of Science*, vol. 28, (1961).

54. Ibid.   *Communication* : *A Logical Model*, The
                     M.I.T. Press, Cambridge, Mass., (1963).

55. Hofstadter, A. & "On the Logic of Imperatives," *Philoso-*
    McKinsey,   *phy of Science*, vol. 6, (1939).
    I.C.C.

56. Hiz, Henry   "Questions and Answers," *Journal of*
                     Philosophy, LIX, no. 10, (1962).

57. Jörgensen, J.   "Imperatives and Logic," *Erkenntnis*, vol.
                     7, (1938).

58. Juarez-Paz, R.   "Reasons, Commands, and Moral Princi-
                     ples," *Logique et Analyse*, vol. 2, (1959).

59. Keene, G.B.   "Can Commands Have Logical Conse-
                     quences ?" *American Philosophical Quar-*
                     terly, vol. 3, (1966).

60. Kim, Jaegwon   "On the Psycho-physical Identity Theory,"
                     American Philosophical Quarterly, vol. 3,
                     (1966).

61. Kotarbinski, T. *Praxiology*, translated by O. Wojasiewicz,
                     Oxford,   New York,   Pergamon Press,
                     1915.

62. Lemmon, E.J.   "Moral Dilemmas," *Philosophical Review*,
                     vol. 71, (1962).

63. Leonard,   "Interogatives, Imperatives, Truth, Falsity,
    Henry S.   and Lies," *Philosophy of Science*, vol. 26,
                     (1959).

64. Ibid.   "Authorship and Purpose," *Philosophy of*
                     Science, vol. 26, (1959).

65. Lewis, C.I.   *An Analysis of Knowledge and Valuation*,
                     La Salle, Illinois, 1946.

66. Ibid.   "The Modes of Meaning," in *Semantics*
                     and the Philosophy of Language, edited by
                     L. Linsky, The University of Illinois Press
                     at Urbana, 1952.

67. Mair, Neinrich   *Die Psychologie des emotiven Denkens*,
                     Tubingen, 1908.

68. Mally, Ernst   *Grundgesetze des Sollens, Elemente der Logik des Sollens*, Leuschner-Lubensky, 1926, Graz.

69. Martin, Richard M.   *Truth and Denotation*, The University of Chicago Press, Chicago (1958).

70. Ibid.   *Towards A Systematic Pragmatics*, North-Holland Publishing Co., Amsterdam (1959).

71. Ibid.   *Intention and Decision*, Prentice-Hall, Englewood Cliffs, New Jersey, (1963).

72. Ibid.   "Performance, Purpose, and Permission," *Philosophy of Science*, vol. 30, (1963).

73. Ibid.   *Performance*, mimeograph copy.

74. Ibid.   *Events, Histories, Physical Objects : Some Logico-Metaphysical Reflections*, mimeograph copy.

75. Mayo, B. & Mitchell   "The Varieties of Imperatives," *Proceedings of the Aristotelian Society*, Supplementary Volume 31. (1957).

76. McGuire, M.C.   "Can I do what I think I ought not ?" *Mind*, vol. 70 (1961).

77. Meinong, Alexis   *Uber Annahmen*, Leizzig, 1902, 2nd edition, 1910.

78. Menger, Karl   "A Logic of the Doubtful : On Optative and Imperative Logic," *Reports of a Mathematical Colloquium*, Notre Dame University (Indiana) University Press, 2nd series, no. 1, (1939).

79. Ibid.   *Moral Wille und Weltgestaltung*, Wien, 1934.

80. Moore, George E.   *Ethics*, Oxford University Press, 1914.

81. Morris, C.W.   *Signs, Language, and Behavior*, Prentice-Hall, Inc., New York, 1946.

82. Moutafakis,   "Concerning Von Wright's Logic of
    Nicholas J.   Norms," *Philosophy and Phenomenological
                        Research*, Vol. XXXI, June, 1971.

83. Ibid.   "The Extensional Pragmatics of Com-
                        mands," *Notre Dame Journal of Formal
                        Logic*, Vol. XII, No. 4, October, 1971.

84. Ibid.   "A New Approach Towards a Logic of
                        Imperatives," *The Southern Journal of Phi-
                        losophy*, Vol. 9, Winter, 1971, No. 4.

85. Ibid.   "Herbert A. Simon on Imperatives and
                        Heuristic Decision Making," *The Modern
                        Schoolman*, (Jan. 1975).

86. Ibid.   "Towards an Analysis of Erotetic Com-
                        munication," *The Notre Dame Journal of
                        Formal Logic*, (Forthcoming 1975).

87. Peters, A.F.   "R.M. Hare on Imperative Sentences,"
                        Mind, vol. 58, (1949).

88. Prior, Arthur N.   *Formal Logic*, Oxford University Press,
                        2nd ed., London, 1962.

89. Ibid.   *Logic and Basis of Ethics*, Oxford Univer-
                        sity Press, London, 1949.

90. Prior, Mary   "Erotetic Logic," *Philosophical Review*,
    Laura   vol. LXIV, (1955).

91. Quine, Willard   *Word and Object*, M.I.T. Press and John
    V.O.   Wiley & Sons, Inc., New York and Lon-
                        don, (1960).

92. Ibid.   *From A Logical Point of View*, 2nd ed.
                        Harper & Row, New York (1963).

93. Rescher, N. and   "Can One Infer Commands From Com-
    Robinson, J.   mands ?" *Analysis*, vol. 25 (1965).

94. Rescher,   *The Logic of Commands*, Dover Publica-
    Nicholas   tions, Inc., New York, (1966).

95. Ross, Alf   "Imperatives and Logic," *Philosophy of
                        Science*, vol. 11 (1944).

96. Russell,   *An Inquiry Into Meaning and Truth*, Nor-
    Bertrand   ton, New York (1940).

97. Ibid.   *Logic and Knowledge*, ed. R C. Marsch,
                     Allen and Unwin, London (1956).

98. Sagerstedt, T.T. "Imperative Propositions and Judgments
                     of Value," *Theoria*, vol. 11, (1945).

99. Sellars, W.   "Pure Pragmatics and Epistemology,"
                     Philosophy of Science, vol. 14, (1947).

100. Ibid.   "Realism and the New Way of Words,"
                     in H. Feigl and W. Sellars *Readings in
                     Philosophical Analysis*, Appleton-Century-
                     Crofts, Inc., 1949.

101. Ibid.   "Imperatives, Intensions, and the Logic
                     of "Ought'," in *Morality and the Langu-
                     age of Conduct*, ed. by Castaneda and
                     G. Nakhnikian, Wayne University Press,
                     Detroit (1963).

102. Simon, Herbert "The Logic of Rational Decision," *The
     A.   British Journal for the Philosophy of
                     Science*, vol. XVI. November, 1965 no.
                     63.

103. Ibid.   "The Logic of Heuristic Decision Mak-
                     ing," in N. Rescher, ed., *The Logic of
                     Decision and Action*, University of Pitts-
                     burg Press, 1967.

104. Ibid.   *The Science of the Artificial*, M.I.T. Press,
                     1970.

105. Smiley, T.J.   "The Logical Basis of Ethics," *Acta Phi-
                     losophica Fennica*, fasc. 16, (1963).

106. Stevenson, C.L. *Ethics and Language*, Yale University
                     Press, New Haven (1944).

107. Storer, Thomas "The Logic of Value Imperatives," *Philo-
                     sophy of Science*, vol. 13. (1946).

108. Strawson, P.F. "Truth," *Proceedings of the Aristotlelian
                     Society*, Supplementary Volume 24 (1950).

109. Tarski, Alfred   "The Semantic Conception of Truth," in
                       H. Feigel and W. Sellars *Readings in Philosophical
                       Analysis*, Appleton-Century-
                       Crofts, Inc., 1949.

110. Turnbull, R.G.   A Note on R.M. Hare's 'Logic of Imperatives',"
                       Philosophical Analysis vol. 5
                       (1954).

111. Von Wright,
     G.H.   "Deontic Logic," *Mind*, vol. 60 (1951).

112. Ibid.   "On the Logic of Some Axiological and
                       Epistemological Concepts," *Ajatus*, vol.
                       17 (1952).

113. Ibid.   *Norm and Action*, Routledge and Kegan
                       Paul, London, (1963).

114. Williams,   "Imperative Inference," *Analysis Supplement*,
     B.A.O.   1963 (for volume 23).

INDEX